AF235181

Narcissists at Work

Also by Dr Sarah Davies

How to Leave a Narcissist ... For Good
Raised by Narcissists

Narcissists at Work

How to Navigate Difficult People and Workplace Toxicity

DR SARAH DAVIES

SOUVENIR
PRESS

First published in Great Britain in 2026 by
Souvenir Press,
an imprint of Profile Books Ltd
29 Cloth Fair
London
EC1A 7JQ

www.souvenirpress.co.uk

Copyright © Dr Sarah Davies, 2026

The information, advice and techniques presented in this book are based on the
author's experience and research and are accurate to the best of the author's knowledge
at the time of writing. This book is intended for information purposes only and
is not intended as a diagnosis or treatment, and it does not constitute
medical, psychological or legal advice.

Every individual's circumstances are unique. Readers are encouraged to consult with
qualified healthcare professionals, therapists or legal advisors regarding any personal concerns
or before making decisions related to their health, well-being or legal matters.

The author and publisher accept no responsibility for any loss, injury or harm,
adverse effect or consequence resulting from any use of any suggestions or content in
this book. The reader assumes full responsibility for their actions and outcomes.

Names and details of case studies outlined in this book are for illustrative purposes only.

1 3 5 7 9 10 8 6 4 2

Typeset by CC Book Production

Printed and bound in Great Britain by
CPI Group (UK) Ltd, Croydon, CR0 4YY

The moral right of the author has been asserted.

All rights reserved. Without limiting the rights under copyright reserved above, no
part of this publication may be reproduced, stored or introduced into a retrieval system,
or transmitted, in any form or by any means (electronic, mechanical, photocopying,
recording or otherwise), without the prior written permission of both the
copyright owner and the publisher of this book.

Profile Books takes seriously the responsibility of defending our authors' copyright.
No part of this book may be used or reproduced in any manner for the purpose of
training artificial intelligence technologies or systems (including but not limited to
machine learning models and large language models (LLMs)). In accordance with
Article 4(3) of the DSM Directive 2019/790, Profile Books expressly reserves
this work from the text and data mining exception.

A CIP catalogue record for this book is available from the British Library.

Our product safety representative in the EU is BGC Sustainability & Compliance,
7 avenue du Général Leclerc, Paris, 75014, France https://baldwinglobalconsulting.com

ISBN 978 1 80522 623 9
eISBN 978 1 80522 625 3

MIX
Paper | Supporting
responsible forestry
FSC
www.fsc.org
FSC® C013604

To my loved ones, for your support, encouragement and humour.

To my clients, past and present, whose honesty, courage and resilience have been among my greatest teachers.

And to you and every reader seeking hope and healing – may these pages bring you comfort and remind you of your own strength.

Contents

PART 3:
SHIELDING FROM NARCISSISTS AT WORK

PART 4:
MOVING FORWARD

Appendix

Introduction

If you've reached for this book, you may be having a hard time at work, and you may suspect you know the cause. Perhaps you do a good job, work hard and can honestly say you show up each day willing and ready to do your best and get on with your co-workers and your boss. But something is wrong and, despite what you do, perhaps there is someone, or a few people, who don't show up for work in the same way, and that creates a toxic environment. Do you suspect you are working with, or for a narcissist?

You may have already seen my previous self-help books on narcissism and recovery from narcissistic abuse: *How to Leave a Narcissist for Good*, which focuses on ending personal toxic relationship patterns, and *Raised by Narcissists*, which looks at parental narcissism and offers advice on navigating narcissism within the family.

Narcissists at Work explores narcissism and specifically covers how to deal with narcissists in the workplace. Here, I want to share my personal experience within the workplace as well as my thoughts from having professionally specialised in this area for many years.

I wanted this book to address narcissism within professional settings, which is a very real and often overlooked problem that so many people are faced with. Despite changes over recent years and shifts in awareness of workplace well-being and the duty that companies have towards their employees' mental health, toxic work environments remain prevalent. It is perhaps no surprise that there are such high rates of work-related stress, illness and burnout. There are many root causes of unhealthy, toxic situations and relationships, but I'm going to address narcissistic business owners, managers, colleagues, and even clients, who can all have a huge effect on everyone around them. While we may have some choice about where we work and how we work, we can't always control *who* we work with, including the colleagues, customers or clients we may have to interact with. However, you *can* work on developing a whole range of protective practices that help safeguard not only you and your own well-being, but also your career. This can also help you to navigate finding a healthier work environment.

I'll cover an understanding of the origins and nature of narcissism and Narcissistic Personality Disorder, as well as narcissistic defences, specific behaviours and abuse. Then, explore current understandings and discuss the prevalence of narcissism in our society and in certain industries, and consider some of the possible reasons for this. I'll explain how narcissism can present in a range of work environments and share how you can identify it. We will look at how narcissism impacts those who encounter it and, crucially, what you can do to manage this. Throughout the book I will offer a practical and pragmatic guide to help you feel more confident and comfortable in dealing with difficult, toxic and narcissistic people in your own professional life.

My Experience

To write this book, I bring in my many years' experience as a counselling psychologist and trauma therapist specialising in treating those who have experienced narcissistic abuse. However, I also draw from my earlier career in recruitment and head-hunting. In particular, I worked for many years helping start-ups to build a core, foundational team of the right mix of people. This involved understanding psychology; from people's motivation and values to their learning, communication and working styles. Fundamentally, I've always believed that successful teams are built from employing people with a wide and varied mix of skillsets, who also share the same values. Usually, in successful companies, their values and vision are clear.

This, I believe, is key to an effective and positive workforce. In my experience, the start-ups that would go on to become successful were particular right from the early stages about getting the core team and ethos right. There would typically be the odd, slightly eccentric techy, a charismatic sales director, a pedantic finance controller and a solid and grounded administration and operations lead. There would also be different personalities and interests and senses of humour, but that didn't matter so much; if everyone more or less shared a common clear vision and important core values, like honesty, trustworthiness, supportiveness and reliability, the growth was largely harmonious. Wherever there were huge, unmanageable egos, power struggles, conflicts of values or interests, or greed or bullying, it was inevitably a hopeless and futile, troublesome and, needless to say, highly stressful – if not traumatic – experience.

I became very interested in the personality profiling and psychological aspect of recruitment and business and so began my studies into human psychology. I took a degree in psychology and then trained and qualified as a chartered counselling psychologist. I've since undertaken further training in trauma therapy, body-based approaches, nutritional and nutrient therapy. I continue to study yoga, yogic psychology and meditation. I have always believed in taking a holistic view of our overall mental health and well-being.

When I first began studying psychology, narcissism was not really being discussed in the mainstream. There wasn't a great deal of information or awareness about it. This has changed so much since I began working and ultimately specialising in this area.

Clients I saw before the recent boom in awareness rarely came to therapy seeking help specifically for the impact of narcissism or narcissistic abuse, or even naming it as such – in fact, most people had never heard of narcissistic abuse. Instead, clients would come to ask for help to find ways to be a 'better' partner or employee. They would typically present with low self-esteem or confidence and were essentially seeking help to become 'better', 'enough' or 'good enough' at work. After exploring further, it would become apparent that my clients' issues stemmed from that difficult-to-please person in their life – the narcissist – and it was the narcissist who was causing them to feel 'less than', convincingly enough to make my clients believe they needed to be better for *them*.

Ultimately, nothing you ever do is enough or will ever be good enough for a narcissist.

That's not personal. That's the dynamic.

That's just the deal with any impossible-to-please narcissist.

So very early on in my clinical work as a psychologist, I became interested in recognising toxic dynamics and their impact on the people who came to see me. Many clients who were struggling with stress, burnout, anxiety or depression, or additional maladaptive and unhealthy coping strategies like using alcohol, abusing prescription/recreational drugs or food, would reveal a toxic relationship in their lives.

Being in any kind of a relationship with a personality-disordered, controlling, emotionally manipulative, exploitative toxic person is obviously going to take its toll and leave most people feeling stressed, triggered, anxious, stuck, trapped or being pushed to an edge. In extreme cases I've seen people pushed to complete nervous breakdown. I've also seen many people become quickly restored to sanity, well-being and peace once they come away from such abusive relationships.

Awareness is key.

Being aware of and informed about narcissism and narcissistic abuse is a key first step to addressing the harm it can do to you. Understanding what it is you're dealing with and why you might be thinking or feeling the way you do is an important shift, especially when it comes to understanding narcissism and the impacts of being around it. Arming yourself with accurate and helpful information is the first step towards a new sense of growth, recovery and freedom.

One of the reasons I quickly recognised this in clients when I started working as a practitioner psychologist was because I recognised the signs and symptoms from my own experience: I grew up around narcissism and dysfunctional relationships in my family. However, like many children growing up with this, I didn't know it at the time, and so, unsurprisingly, replicated a similar relationship dynamic in my personal adult relationships and even at work. And so I began my own journey of healing and recovery from narcissistic abuse. My own experience has really helped inform my clinical practice.

A Unique View

I've spent much of my clinical experience working with people of prominence and status. This includes working at some of the world's most exclusive, pioneering private treatment centres, as well as in my Harley Street practice in London.

The treatment centres I worked for were unique. They were some of the first of their kind to provide a truly individualised, elite private service for high-end addiction and mental health treatment. They offered a holistic approach and had a vision of always seeking to treat a person's underlying trauma – a view that I maintain to this day. These treatment centres were highly sophisticated and luxurious, the kind of set-up that charged £100,000 per week for their services. For this, uber-wealthy clients could expect a 24/7 live-in therapist while staying in a luxury 5+ star residence, with a private chef, maid, personal chauffeur and security to hand. A specialist team of doctors, medics, psychologists, holistic therapists and trainers would then work around the clock with them in a uniquely tailored way. It's obviously a highly niche area with an impressive approach and concept.

Coming from a humble background myself, I had from time to time fantasised, like a lot of people do, about how great and easy it must be to be super rich. But during my time working in this area I soon saw that this is far from the case. For many people, more wealth or fame can mean more problems, especially when it comes to narcissism-related issues. I learnt a lot during this time, not only about holistic and trauma treatment but also about working with narcissism and the knock-on effects from being around narcissistic abuse.

I'm not saying that all rich or famous people are narcissistic – of course not. However, there are certainly areas of life and sectors where you will find a higher population of narcissistic people and therefore related narcissistic abuse. Arguably, there is an element of narcissism that for some people is a part of their seeking fame or power. Narcissists will also flock to be around or associated with any kind of celebrity or status like a moth to a flame.

Whether in my work I was meeting people with strong narcissistic traits or their victims (be it partners, parents or business-related associates), stories of being used, taken advantage of in one way or another or of being conned out of money or assets, emotionally manipulated in relationships, used and gaslighted were rife. Experiencing narcissistic abuse is a distinct form of psychological abuse. And it's one that is traumatic and deeply impactful.

Wherever there is power, status or wealth, there will be narcissists. And wherever there are narcissists, there will usually be some degree of manipulation, control or abuse.

I've found it incredible to see how wealth or status can change some people. There will always be manipulative vultures trying to get what they can wherever there is money, status or power. You've only got to look to Hollywood to see this. Greed and envy are toxic. But narcissists are pathologically focused on obtaining or being linked to status, wealth or power in any way they can, and this goes for all industries and sectors across the world and at all levels of income.

A Shift in Awareness

When I returned from working overseas in 2016, I set up a private practice in London working with people who had experienced narcissistic abuse, toxic relationships, anxiety, stress, burnout and trauma.

Around the same time, there was a rapidly emerging shift in the discussion of narcissism in the mainstream. This was perhaps reflective of what was happening culturally in the world at that time. Suddenly the word 'narcissist' was being used a lot more. Only a few years prior to then, if you googled the term 'narcissistic abuse' just a handful of results would come up; now it's over a billion.

From this time, I started to meet more and more people who were seeking therapy specifically for help with narcissistic abuse. At that point, too, there were just a handful of therapists specialising in this area in the UK. The buzz around narcissism really captured and gained interest. A few years later, in 2022, Merriam-Webster Dictionary named *'gaslighting'* as their word of the year, following a 1,740 per cent increase in internet searches for the term.

With many mental health issues, this kind of increase in public awareness and understanding can be a helpful shift. Conversely, it can also mean that terms become overused and subsequently misunderstood. I think that the clinical definition of narcissism tends to get a little lost when the term is bandied around in the way it has been in recent years. You will also find on the internet and across social media a lot of misinformation and anecdotal cases that may not necessarily be clinically accurate or reliable. My advice is to be discerning about whose opinion and guidance you trust.

It means everything to me to be able to use my personal journey of recovery as well as my professional experience to help support others to heal and move on from this and, what's more, to find freedom and strength from what can otherwise be a truly horrific experience.

This is a comprehensive guide to recognising and moving on from narcissism and narcissists, combining expert advice, personal experience and case studies. The case studies included draw upon my professional work, but they are solely intended to illustrate common patterns and dynamics; they do not represent any specific individual, organisation or workplace.

I genuinely hope *Narcissists at Work* will enable you to recognise narcissism and provide you with the practical tools to navigate these difficult relationships. My wish is that it also helps you to develop the self-care practices and the loving, trusting relationship with yourself that you need to make the right decisions for you – both now and in the future.

Wishing you the very best.

Dr Sarah Davies

PART ONE:

UNDERSTANDING NARCISSISM

1

How to Recognise Narcissism

Understanding narcissism helps you to recognise difficult personalities and toxic dynamics, in your personal and professional life. This can be protective not just for your mental health, but for your professional well-being and career.

Before we examine the specifics of encountering a narcissistic boss or colleague at work, let's look at narcissistic personalities generally. The core traits of this remain the same across different relationships and situations. The workplace context shapes how these traits manifest, or how they're rewarded or concealed.

In everyday life, you might choose to distance yourself from a narcissistic friend or family member. But at work, we don't always have that choice. The workplace often provides narcissists with a perfect platform: hierarchy, competition, validation, recognition, measurable markers of 'success', admiration, status... all the ingredients they seek for their insatiable ego.

Understanding their behaviours and tactics will help you to see through the facade with clarity rather than confusion. When you recognise the patterns, you stop questioning yourself and instead can start protecting yourself.

Narcissism and the concept of extreme selfishness and self-interest has existed for a long, long time; however, as we've seen, in more recent years there has been a shift towards more widespread understanding and awareness of it. At the same time, aspects of modern-day culture breed more of it.

The term 'narcissist' originates from the tragic tale of Narcissus and Echo in Greek mythology. The story goes that Echo, a mountain nymph, had her freedom of speech taken from her as punishment for being overly talkative. She was left only able to repeat others' last words. One day Echo spotted Narcissus, a hunter known for his beauty, and became infatuated by his looks and charm. She attempted to embrace him and Narcissus rejected her, as he had many others. As punishment for his vanity and cruel rejection, Nemesis, goddess of revenge, laid a curse upon him so he would fall in love with, yet never be loved by, the next person his eyes fell upon. While hunting one day he became thirsty and, reaching down to a pool of water to drink, saw and fell in love with his own reflection. He became infatuated with this image and was trapped in the lifelong, futile pursuit of obtaining this unobtainable love. Echo, meanwhile, continued in vain to try to win his attention and affections. She was left only able to repeat the last words of others.

From this story we can understand how narcissists are inherently self-obsessed and cannot truly see or connect with others. Those around them, like Echo, can lose themselves in the process of trying to connect with them or win their approval. You may relate to this if you are or suspect you are working with a narcissist. Understanding this story can be useful in helping you to recognise the futility of trying to gain genuine recognition or connection from a narcissist, as well as the importance of preserving your own voice.

Before we get into exploring in more detail why there is so much awareness and fascination with narcissism in the mainstream now and how it presents in the workplace, let's go through the clinical definition of Narcissistic Personality Disorder (NPD) and how you can learn to recognise it. This includes the characteristics, behaviours and relational patterns linked to narcissism and explores more about why people are narcissistic.

What Is Narcissism?

Clinical narcissism is a complex personality issue that reflects long-held patterns of thinking and behaviour. It's a deep and long-term trait that typically starts to develop during childhood and is present by adulthood. It is significantly impactful on mental and emotional well-being and relationships.

The *DSM* is a diagnostic manual used by specialist clinicians to help identify psychiatric and mental health disorders. In the *DSM-5*, Narcissistic Personality Disorder (NPD) is described as a long-term condition characterised by: *a pervasive pattern of grandiosity (in fantasy or behaviour), a need for admiration and lack of empathy.*

Related psychological and behavioural patterns begin by early adulthood and are evident across a variety of contexts. NPD is further indicated by possessing and demonstrating at least five of the following characteristics:

- **Grandiose sense of self-importance:** People with NPD expect special treatment and possess a need to be recognised as superior to others. In order to position themselves as better or more important, they may exaggerate or lie about, for example, themselves, their lives or their achievements or skills.
- **Need for admiration:** There is a pathological need for admiration or attention.
- **Lack of empathy:** People with NPD do not experience empathy in the way that non-narcissistic people do. They are therefore unable to recognise, be genuinely affected by or care about the feelings or needs of others.
- **Preoccupied with 'success':** They have fantasies and ideas of power, success, wealth, brilliance, beauty or love.
- **A belief of being special and unique:** They believe that they can only be understood by other 'special' people or institutions, and so deserve to be associated with or connected to them.
- **Strong sense of entitlement:** Narcissists have unrealistic expectations of how they should be treated. They also expect others to comply with their expectations, wants or demands even though they won't consider anyone else's (due to their lack of ability to experience empathy).
- **Envious:** They are envious of others and/or believe that others are envious or jealous of them.

- **Arrogant:** They display arrogant, haughty behaviours or attitudes.

- **Interpersonally exploitative:** They manipulate and take advantage of others in a variety of ways to achieve their own selfish and self-seeking wants and goals.

For truly narcissistic people, their worldview and perspective really centre around themselves. They are fundamentally focused on their own wants and needs. They don't tend to consider much beyond that.

Because of these diagnostic characteristics and the fact that the narcissistic mind is so self-focused and self-interested, narcissistic people do not have the ability to engage in healthy and meaningful relationships. They are very limited in their capacity to connect with and care about others in an authentic or genuine way. Instead, they view others through a lens of *'what can this person do for me?'*. Understandably then, they tend to favour those who can offer them any kind of gains or advantage to help get them to where they want to be. This could be contacts, wealth or status. It could be anyone who is willing to give them enough admiration or attention, or be impressed or in awe of them enough to constantly boost their fragile egos. It may be that somebody else is willing or able to assume some level of responsibility for, or otherwise to enable, their actions. They look for people they can control and manipulate. They prefer to employ or work with people with loose boundaries or who may not stand up to them or try to hold them accountable. They like to surround themselves with their own fan club.

'My boss always takes credit for all my hard work – yet I never get a thanks or even any acknowledgement!' Rob

The core clinical features of Narcissistic Personality Disorder are: selfishness, distinct lack of empathy and the range of self-seeking behaviours and characteristics outlined above. In terms of how this presents, broadly speaking, you will see and can learn to recognise two main types of narcissism: overt and covert.

Overt/Grandiose Narcissism

An overt narcissist is the more stereotypical, most easily recognised grandiose presentation of narcissism. In fact, once you understand what narcissism is and see this, it's hard to miss it.

The grandiose kind of narcissist is the one most commonly portrayed in films and TV and you may recognise it among certain celebrities or politicians. You will also see it in the medical and business worlds.

The overt narcissist exudes a kind of magnetic energy. They tend to be attractive, confident, charming and charismatic. You will notice that people are unwittingly drawn to them. You may even experience that powerful pull yourself. Overt narcissists come across as self-assured and arrogant and are enigmatically persuasive. They absolutely thrive on power and control, both in and out of the workplace. As such, it's not unusual to find them in places and positions of power. This could be in business, law, politics, the medical field, the charity sector or academia, to name a few. You will see this on social media with certain influencers too. Wherever there is a position of power, a master-to-student or guru–follower type of dynamic you will find narcissistic people. They want to be in position to exert knowledge, power and control, and have a pathological need for a following. They don't experience themselves as equal... to anybody. The overt kinds particularly thrive on an explicit power dynamic over others.

One of the most compelling portrayals of an overt narcissistic boss in business I've seen is the character Logan Roy in the TV series *Succession*, brilliantly portrayed by Brian Cox. Logan is the head of a multimillion-dollar business empire and basically rules and controls everybody in his life – personally and professionally – through fear, manipulation and intimidation. He is bullish, rude, ruthless and brutal. He couldn't care less who or what he harms in pursuit of his own grand ambitions – even if those people are partners or family or anyone else who has shown him loyalty over time. Driven by money and greed, he emotionally manipulates and exploits all those around him. He constantly plays off his children against one another, creating mistrust, paranoia, rivalry and division between them. The same is true for all those who work for him. A liar and a cheat, he controls all those around him. He does all of the above with zero empathy or remorse. He refuses to accept that he has flaws or weaknesses, instead slamming anyone and everyone around him for being weak or below par. He is highly aggressive and volatile and has a habit of marking the end of meetings by shouting at somebody to 'f*** off'. (Narcissists are not good with endings!) As overt narcissist types are usually found in positions of power, they are ultimately more likely to be managers or business owners, or in another position of power, whether in a one-to-one setting or a group. The scope for this is vast; businesspeople, doctors, psychiatrists, lawyers, investors, financial controllers, politicians, spiritual/healthcare gurus and so on. The behaviours and abuse of the overt narcissist are easier to spot than the more covert types. Overt narcissistic bosses or colleagues tend to be more suave and polished. They will dress well and look good (looks and image are important to them). Overt narcissistic abuse is usually unashamedly obvious and direct. Overt narcissists will criticise, judge, shout, shame, ignore and undermine people directly. They set up alliances and division among colleagues and create a culture of mistrust, competitiveness, insecurity and paranoia. Needless to say, it's incredibly stressful to deal with all this at work.

At the same time, they can possess a mystical-like charm to get away with what they do and in the way that they do it. A part of their manipulation is to seduce and compliment those they see as being able to serve them in some way. They have an innate ability to seek out these people. Narcissists make those unsuspecting parties feel 'special', by giving them all sorts of compliments, and making them promises and declarations. The most narcissistic people experience others as commodities. They want to charm and manipulate others in order to get what they want. As soon as they believe somebody no longer serves them in the way that benefits them, they will easily drop them like a hot potato and behave as if they never existed, before swiftly moving on to somebody else. They are compelled to find the next person who may be fooled by their allure and deceptions, or who is more willing at that time to give them what they want. They have the power to make a person feel wonderful, and to abuse and destroy.

The way narcissists view and treat people is one of the reasons why narcissism is so detrimental in a work setting. It is ultimately futile to strive to please an impossible-to-please narcissistic boss or colleague. Nothing is ever enough for any kind of narcissist. They won't ever sincerely care about your well-being. The narcissistic boss will run their staff into the ground and, the moment anyone experiences burnout or reaches a limit, they simply drop them, lose interest and replace them with the next person. It is not personal. It's just what they do. They are wired in such a way as to serve their own pursuits.

Mark's experience:

I remember the first meeting I had with the owner of a rapidly growing company I was super keen to work for. I knew he was very successful. He was larger than life. When I walked into the room to introduce myself, I remember feeling like he completely filled the room with his charisma and personality. I felt lucky to be in his presence. He was tall, good-looking, dressed immaculately, had a very nice watch, shoes, and smelt great. It's a little embarrassing to admit now, but I just really wanted to be around him. I was greeted with his beaming, perfect smile and honestly... I felt great in his company. I felt like we had an instant connection. In hindsight, I realise it was actually quite an unusual interview, but at the time I was swept away in the excitement of it all. Rather than ask me many questions about myself or my skills or experience, he talked all about himself. He relished sharing how he'd come to set up and run his successful business – and was certainly not shy about saying how successful it was. He told me how he'd managed this against the odds and how certain people along the way had tried to sabotage and destroy his efforts. It really was quite a journey and I was captivated by his stories. During the 'interview' – if you can really call it that – I remained interested and engaged and, truth be told, was in awe of all he had accomplished. I came away feeling not only positive, but elated. He firmly shook my hand and said his PA would be in touch. I was promptly offered the job and was excited to start.

Within eight months of joining the firm, my job was truly a living nightmare. I had walked straight into an unbelievably toxic work culture, full of false promises and lies. I saw – more clearly in hindsight – that the owner enjoyed pitting his employees against each other in any which way and, as a result, many of the staff were competing against one another in order to please and be his 'favourite'. This created a culture of rivalry and mistrust and some colleagues seemed compelled to highlight one another's mistakes or draw attention to anybody leaving on time. If any staff did something that was unsatisfactory to him, instead of discussing this in any kind of appropriate way there would be shouting and roaring to be heard throughout the office. Everybody there worked in fear of losing their job. It was incredibly stressful. I was scared to make a mistake. Very quickly I became stressed, anxious, overworked and on the verge of burnout. I wasn't sleeping well and felt paranoid and scared at work. In retrospect the signs were there from the interview, but I absolutely got caught up

in the excitement and charm of him and how things were
presented. And quickly paid the price.

Overt narcissists in the workplace are blatant in their behaviours and attitudes. They are often found in positions of power, where they can bully, manipulate and control others. If they have not quite reached the top, then they are certainly on their way to getting there. The overt types need that sense of authority and power. They thrive on drama and conflict.

Covert/Vulnerable Narcissism

Covert narcissists, while sharing the same core pathology as overt types, are much more subtle in their display, behaviours, emotional manipulation and actions. Covert narcissism is otherwise referred to as 'vulnerable' or 'introverted' narcissism, so unlike the bolder, attention- and power-seeking grandiose overt display, covert narcissists in comparison tend to be quieter, more softly spoken and unassuming. They can appear vulnerable, friendly, helpful or caring, humble, self-sacrificing or altruistic. However, in time you may also see signs that this is disingenuous and reflective of their subtle means of manipulating and sophisticated ways to control or to get what they want from others at work. You can learn to recognise covert narcissism through observing patterns of behaviour.

The aim of either type of narcissist is ultimately to cater to and serve their own selfish wishes and desires. A covert narcissist, though, will be more willing to share or portray signs of their own insecurities, flaws, weaknesses or vulnerabilities. They can appear sensitive, self-deprecating or troubled. In my experience, I've found that covert narcissists are masterful at turning up at a time where another person is, for whatever reason, vulnerable. Many clients I have worked with over the years will also share that a covert narcissist arrived at a difficult time, 'like a knight in shining armour', and their initial support was welcome. However, in time, it becomes apparent that this is often essentially an information-gathering exercise for them in trying to understand your thoughts or ideas; later they will try to use this against you in whatever way they can. Their initial offers of help are often only recognised later as them having orchestrated some kind of dependence or control or manipulation. Again, this all ultimately serves them to get their own needs met.

Rather than being explicitly loud and aggressive like overt narcissists, covert or vulnerable narcissists tend to be more passive-aggressive. They often present as victims; sometimes this is perpetual. A good way to recognise this trait in colleagues is to look out for the person who always seems to have a problem going on in their lives or at work. They seem to enjoy having and sharing their problems. These may be about work, the boss, the clients, other colleagues, or they may bring in personal issues to bend your ear about. Sharing concerns, problems or gossip is a way in which a covert narcissist seeks to get their narcissistic supply – in other words, it's an effective way to create a fairly constant stream of attention and support from others. However, you may notice that they rarely, if ever, take any responsibility to do anything helpful or productive. So rather than genuinely seeking advice or a solution, they instead get something from continuously having a problem to complain about. Both kinds of narcissists have a pathological need for validation and admiration, yet the coverts aim to do this by seeking pity, support or a kind ear or fishing for compliments from others.

Covert narcissists try to control others in much less aggressive ways than the overt narcissist. They use gaslighting, guilt-tripping, scaremongering or victimhood tactics to control relationships and maintain some sense of power over others. They also use passive-aggressive communication, including limitation or withdrawal of communication. Silent treatment, short snappy answers, sarcasm, mixed messages and making intentional mistakes are all examples of passive-aggressive communication at work. Despite coming across as meek, supportive or accommodating on the surface, covert narcissists are just as manipulative in their ability to exploit others to meet their needs.

Some behavioural patterns that can present in the workplace of covert narcissism include:

Being perpetual victims: This is the colleague who positions themselves as the victim, in either a professional, relational or personal sense. They will habitually seek out somebody who will listen and empathise with them about how they've been poorly treated, misunderstood or undervalued by a person or organisation. They often want to get into criticising or gossiping about management, colleagues or some situation at work. This is also the colleague who comes into work to share about yet another story from their personal life. Narcissists thrive on drama and conflict. Covert narcissists can come across like genuine victims and are comfortable portraying themselves as such; however, you may spot that there is an ongoing pattern of this kind of behaviour. Often this manifests as patterns of perpetual victimhood and a preference for complaining, rather than taking any positive action to ever change anything. Their 'suffering' provides a function for them to get the attention they want and need.

Silent sabotage: This is the kind of covert narcissist who appears to be a pleasant and helpful colleague, yet will quietly undermine others in the team. They will withhold information or sabotage projects and at the same time deny any wrongdoing and maintain their innocence. They will insist they tried to help and instead blame somebody or something else for the issue. Again, this is often done in such a subtle, non-confrontational way that it's difficult for others to hold them accountable. Of course, we can all make mistakes; however, in someone who is a narcissist you may notice habits of repeated behaviours, rather than an occasional genuine error.

Passive-aggressiveness: Rather than communicating effectively or actively seeking to resolve any issues in an open or honest way, covert narcissists will engage in passive-aggressive ways of being. This can include short, snappy communication, appearing polite but not really saying what they mean, giving backhanded compliments or harbouring resentments. They are the colleague who will arrive late, be disruptive, move around or eat during meetings, and find other ways to non-verbally communicate their disdain and disinterest.

Oversensitivity: Covert narcissists often have strong emotional reactions to any kind of feedback, perceiving it as criticism even when it is constructive. Their emotional reactions are manipulative and are intended to make it very difficult for managers or colleagues to relay any real feedback to them. Sometimes other people at work fear or avoid doing so in order to minimise the risk of outbursts. This is 'objective achieved' as far as a manipulative person at work is concerned.

Interpersonal manipulation: Covert narcissists use subtle manipulation to align with certain people in the organisation and find ways to create alliances and division in order to meet their own personal or professional goals. This can include a version of 'love-bombing' where they might shower colleagues with compliments or gifts or future-faking (promises about future training or promotion opportunities) to get people onside and to appear like a friend. Usually when this kind of behaviour feels icky and manipulative... it's because it is. Trust your inner sense.

Natalie's experience:

My manager Tara knocked on my office door with that familiar wounded expression... 'I hate to bother you,' she says, 'I know you're busy but I'm really drowning here...' She looks fragile and stressed and explains how the board are breathing down her neck about the quarterly report. She says, 'I honestly don't think I can handle this at the moment – my anxiety is through the roof.' I feel a familiar tug of guilt and find myself asking, 'What do you need?' Tara quickly replies, 'Can you do the data analysis? I know it's not your job but you're so much better at it than I am. I just can't let down the team again.'

And so I find myself agreeing to do her work for her, again. Tara is relieved, while I am full of dread. I know in that moment I will need to be working over the weekend to get it done. I'm also confused and resentful that I've somehow agreed to do something I could really do without. Tara has yet again masterfully transformed her poor planning into my emergency, all while making me feel like the hero rescuing her from her own incompetence!

While covert narcissism is more subtle than the garish grandiose, overt kind, you can start to recognise these craftier traits and behaviours and spot the signs early on. The sooner you foster more direct and open communication and set clear boundaries, the easier it is to ultimately manage this kind of person or behaviour.

We will look at more examples of both overt and covert narcissism throughout the book to help build on your understanding and ability to recognise it. And we'll cover practical ideas about communication and boundaries and other ways of dealing with it too.

The Spectrum of Narcissism

Narcissism very much exists on a scale. The full spectrum of narcissism goes from mild and occasional narcissistic behaviours or defences to full-blown Narcissistic Personality Disorder (NPD) and beyond.

At the lower end of the spectrum you will find levels of selfishness that may be occasional or even appropriate. Let's face it, we can all be a bit selfish sometimes. That's perfectly understandable and normal. We may also have a degree of narcissistic defences. These are behaviours that temporarily serve to protect us from feeling too much shame in a particular moment. They are immediate defences that kick in when we might feel embarrassed or ashamed and include, for example, behaviours like denial, anger or blame.

If you ask in the office, 'Who ate all the biscuits?' the culprit might snap back an immediate 'Not me!' This is an impulsive, immediate defence to embarrassment and shame. There is often no time to think or feel too much between an accusation and a defensive response – it is an automatic buffer. What happens next though is more telling about a person...

Somebody at the lower end of the narcissism spectrum might initially deny eating the last of the biscuits, yet in the next breath sigh and hold their hands up and say, 'Sorry! It was me. I didn't mean to... it's just they were so tasty... once I started I just couldn't stop!' They may offer to replace them – because they *feel bad* about what they've done. In this example, this is a person who when faced with a shaming situation has an automatic, immediate defence against it. That's quite normal. Nobody likes to feel embarrassed or ashamed. Importantly though, they can then quickly reflect on their actions, consider the impact of them on others and recognise that lying doesn't sit comfortably with their moral compass. (Note here that non-narcissistic people actually have a moral compass!). They possess the humility to hold their hands up and admit their error, and be honest with themselves and others. They are able to apologise – and mean it. A narcissist is not able to do that. Somebody at the lower end of the spectrum may be able to take accountability and personal responsibility. Narcissistic people higher up the scale cannot reflect on their own actions or consider the impact of that on anyone else. They don't experience that level of empathy. They also don't care.

You will also find at the lower end of the spectrum 'age-appropriate' narcissism. Part of normal childhood development is being egocentric. This is typical in young childhood – usually between the ages of two and seven. At this stage we can only see the world and people in it from our own viewpoint, and find it difficult to consider things from another's perspective. If we think or feel a certain way, we essentially believe that's what others are thinking or feeling too. It's very normal for children to go through this stage of development. Adult narcissists, however, do not progress through these psychological developmental milestones and essentially remain stuck at a point of being consumed by their own internal experiences. Narcissistic personalities are, then, essentially psychologically and emotionally fixated on their own thoughts, feelings, wants and needs and therefore do not acknowledge or consider anybody else's.

A narcissist will assault you with their defences. If you touch on something that triggers something for them, their active defences kick in and they will pummel you with their uncontained emotions – this means they will shame, blame, accuse, criticise etc. It will feel like a punch in the gut. A narcissist will lob their sh*t at you like a hot potato they can't hold – the trick is to just recognise this for what it is and try not to catch or hold on to it. Let it drop – it's not yours, it's theirs.

Normal and Healthy Narcissism

I often hear from worried parents of teenagers, highly concerned that they've raised a raging narcissist. Please rest assured that being self-centred to some degree during the teenage years is totally normal; something that many adolescents go through and grow out of as they develop emotional maturity and reach young adulthood. Supporting and modelling healthy boundaries, a sense of one's personal responsibility and accountability can help this developmental progression.

You might be surprised to learn that there is also a concept of 'healthy narcissism'. The term was originally coined in the 1930s by psychoanalyst Paul Federn, and it is defined as 'a positive sense of self and reflects when a level of self-belief and confidence, drive, leadership and success is used for the greater good'. Healthy narcissism includes the capacity to experience empathy, so can be thought of as being at one end of a spectrum, while the kind of narcissism we will focus on in this book is at the opposite end. That kind of narcissism is far from positive or healthy.

So, on the spectrum of narcissism, at the lower end we find healthy narcissism and age-appropriate narcissism. There is then a space, where I think, if we can be really honest with ourselves (something true narcissists struggle to do), we can all be capable of being a bit selfish or self-focused *sometimes*. This can be understandably and appropriately related to what we might have going on from time to time. The difference here though is that it is short-lived, relevant to a difficult or challenging time, and there is self-awareness about this. Self-awareness of one's own selfishness or selfish thinking or actions or any undesirable trait is key to altering our behaviours. This, and the ability to self-reflect honestly and objectively, is something narcissists further up the scale do not have and cannot do.

Going back to the *'biscuit-thief-in-the-office'* analogy, we see that people toward the higher end of the spectrum of narcissism have a more distorted perspective.

An actual narcissist in the same situation would happily eat all the biscuits and wouldn't care about anybody else having any. They would completely deny that they had eaten them and lie about it. The most narcissistic people may even absolutely believe they did not even eat them. They would believe that somebody else did, or that there were never any biscuits in the first place – because they are unable to tolerate being anywhere close to shame. The real narcissist in the office will eat them all, not consider anyone else, point-blank deny any wrongdoing and then blame and shame, and gaslight you for it. The most abusive will leave you doubting your own perception or reality, and wondering whether you imagined the biscuits and questioning whether you've in fact eaten them yourself and somehow have total amnesia about it. Abusive narcissists basically leave you feeling like it's you, your issues, your fault or like there's something gravely wrong with you. It's wild.

The narcissistic mind rewrites reality.

Looking at the full range of the spectrum, we have at the lower end narcissistic defences with varied individual ability to:

a) self-reflect and be honest with self and others
b) experience genuine empathy and care
c) experience and tolerate remorse, guilt or shame.
d) sustain the motivation to change one's behaviour as a result of a–c.

People higher up the scale at increasing levels of narcissism have less ability to experience or action these important steps towards change. This is why it's difficult, if not impossible, for narcissists to change. I'll explain more about that shortly.

At the very end is the most narcissistic of disordered personalities; those that meet all the diagnostic criteria and have an alarming lack of empathy or capacity for genuine self-reflection or awareness. Just to note, beyond this are sociopaths and psychopaths. These are disturbed and dangerous people.

Other Personality Types

As we move up and beyond the narcissistic scale, narcissism and associated attitudes and behaviours become more of a pervasive pattern. With long-term, unchangeable attitudes and patterns of behaviour, we see Narcissistic Personality Disorder. On the broader spectrum of pathology, narcissists and those with NPD are highly interpersonally exploitative and manipulative.

Beyond NPD exist sociopaths and psychopaths. There is also antisocial personality disorder (ASPD). It is helpful to know just enough about this to have an awareness of what you may or may not be dealing with at work. These personality types have a distinct and alarming disregard for others and will often violate other people's rights without remorse. The *DSM-5* characterises Antisocial Personality Disorder types as displaying three or more of the following patterns of behaviour:

Failure to conform to social norms or the law.
Being highly deceptive. Lying, using aliases and intentionally conning others for their personal pleasure or profit.

Impulsivity and failure to plan ahead.

Irritability and aggression. Including being violent.

Reckless disregard for safety of self or others.

Consistently irresponsible. Failure to honour work or financial obligations.

Lack of remorse. Those with ASPD are indifferent about hurting, mistreating or stealing from others.

Psychopaths, sociopaths, antisocial personalities and narcissists all share some similar traits, like distinct lack of empathy and regard for others. However, there are also some differences in terms of the subsequent lack of moral compass and lengths they will go to in order to serve their own desires and needs. In those with sociopathic and psychopathic personalities this can get alarmingly disturbing and dangerous. Narcissists are selfish and manipulative and have little regard for the impact of their actions on others. Sociopaths have the same core pathology but additionally are more willing and able to explicitly harm and abuse others in their pursuit of power or success. They tend to do this in more impulsive and reckless ways. Moving into sociopathic and psychopathic psychology and the very extreme end of the spectrum (this is very rare), is where you see highly dangerous antisocial personalities and behaviours. Here there is a complete and utter lack of regard for rules or laws. There is an inability to control their emotions and so they may fly into an aggressive or violent rage. They have a fierce temper. They are fearless and bold and engage in reckless and dangerous behaviours. Sociopaths and psychopaths are usually highly impulsive and unpredictable. You will never know where you stand or be safe with them. Some gain sadistic pleasure from breaking rules, intimidating others, manipulating, controlling, reigning over others or causing others fear or harm.

Antisocial types are highly represented in the prison population as they are more likely to break the law and engage in violent and criminal activity. They are also, however, found in the business world, as their characteristics also lend themselves to being successful in certain entrepreneurial endeavours.

While the prevalence of these kinds of people is estimated to be low in the general population, some studies have shown they make up about 20 per cent of the prison population... and up to around the same percentage among corporate leaders and professionals.

AUTISTIC SPECTRUM DISORDER AND NARCISSISTIC PERSONALITY DISORDER

When considering whether someone could be a narcissist, I think it can also be useful to be informed about Autistic Spectrum Disorder (ASD) as someone who appears rigid or experiences challenges at work caused by ASD may be wrongly and unfairly seen as displaying narcissistic traits. Autism and narcissism are entirely different issues but there can be some overlap in how some of the symptoms present, which I think is important to distinguish.

Autistic Spectrum Disorder is a neurodevelopmental condition that affects how a person thinks, learns, and processes and organises information. It also impacts to varying degrees on social skills, influencing how a person communicates and interacts with others. It usually presents from early childhood; however, many people learn to successfully 'mask' their struggles and reach adulthood before they are diagnosed. Being on the autistic spectrum is not a clearly defined set of rigid symptoms, but rather a range of conditions and challenges across a range of areas to individually varying degrees. Autism can present differently for different people.

Some aspects of neurodivergence are challenging and other aspects bring unique strengths and skills. An autistic person can bring a high level of focus, attention to detail, ability to spot patterns, creative ways of thinking, excellent problem-solving abilities and direct styles of communication to a workplace.

Appearing to Lack Empathy

I have heard people wrongly mistake autism for NPD due to a seeming lack of empathy; however, there is a fundamental difference between the two. People with Autistic Spectrum Disorder do experience empathy and genuine care and consideration, yet may struggle to share this or will show it in different ways. For example, in response to someone experiencing distress, somebody with autism may offer practical suggestions rather than emotional support. This can be misinterpreted as a lack of care or empathy; however, this is far from the case – the autistic mind just thinks differently.

At play is a neurological difference in reading faces, expressions and cues, resulting in the person with autism not recognising an emotion that someone is feeling.

Narcissists, on the other hand, have a distinct lack of empathy. Psychologically and emotionally, they are unable or unwilling to care much about how another person thinks or feels. They can learn to display a kind of cognitive empathy, although they usually master it in order to be emotionally manipulative. It's not the same as genuinely feeling empathy. Narcissists, despite what they might claim, are generally unaffected by and disregard how others feel. People with autism, on the other hand, can experience a high degree of empathy and be highly sensitive.

Following Instructions

This is an area where there can be confusion about what you are potentially dealing with. People with NPD and those with ASD may both struggle when it comes to following instructions at work; however, this is for completely different reasons.

Those on the autistic spectrum may appear to have difficulty following instructions at work, especially if they are vague or the overall goal or purpose is unclear. With clarity, structure and a clear explanation, a person with autism is usually more than happy to crack on and aim to complete a task to the best of their ability.

Narcissists at work, on the other hand, may have no problem understanding the instructions but will disregard them because they 'know best', or they have a strong preference to do it 'their way'. They will disregard other people's views, input and the overall aim of the project in favour of being some kind of special and different maverick. Needless to say, narcissists are not team players!

Communication

Those on the autistic spectrum can be very literal in their communication – I personally find this makes for very healthy, honest and direct communication, the best kind! However, the downside is that they may come across as blunt or socially awkward. Also, having special interests is a characteristic of autism, so you may hear an autistic person talk at great length about themselves or their special subject. This may appear rude or even narcissistic, as it may sound like 'me, me, me'. It can be mistaken for the way a narcissist will repeatedly bring the conversation back to themselves due to their pathological need for the attention and focus to be all on them at all times.

However, the difference, again, is in the intention. An autistic person has a neurological difference and, if you share something about yourself, they will relate that back to themselves and then share something about their own experience as a way to express understanding and to connect. It's a well-intentioned, mutual communication.

Narcissists, however, tend to take it one step further when talking about themselves or relating a conversation back to them. This is usually done with some kind of bragging, 'topping' or name-dropping. You will find there is a flavour of 'I am better or more important' thrown into the conversation.

Narcissists use communication to manipulate. They can be charming, persuasive, condescending, haughty or passive to get their own way, and, due to their lack of empathy, they'll have little regard for how their communication style impacts others. Autistic people on the other hand will often feel terrible if they are made aware that they have come across as rude. With self-awareness and a motivation to change, those with autism are more likely to try to work on themselves and make positive changes in this regard, whereas a narcissist won't.

Interpersonal Preferences at Work

Autism can present very differently from one person to the next, but generally speaking autistic people tend to prefer autonomy and flexibility at work. As described earlier, there is usually a strong preference for role definition and clarity as well as clear instructions. Many autistic people value routine and straightforward, honest communication and relationships.

This could be misconstrued as being the same as how narcissists prefer to do things their way – only they do it out of a need to be in control. Toxic people will bend or break rules and are inherently drawn to push boundaries in some way. Emotionally manipulative and exploitative at work, narcissists will communicate in unhealthy, indirect, vague, non-committal, undermining and abusive ways.

Possessing Unique Skills and Talents

Many of the world's problems would not be solved without the creative ways of thinking of an autistic mind. Someone with autism can bring innovative problem-solving skills, strong analytical abilities, unique attention to detail and accuracy, an ability to spot patterns and troubleshoot, strong focus and persistence.

Similarly, the more grandiose, overt kinds of narcissists can be mavericks in a positive way in their own right, with the boldness, confidence, self-belief and determination to make the choices that achieve successful outcomes. This is evident in the political and business worlds.

Both can display talent and ability, but the difference is that narcissists rarely achieve success without some trail of upset, bullying or abuse.

Considerations

It is of course possible for somebody to have an overlap and be both autistic and narcissistic. Either way, there are toxic narcissistic behaviours that are simply not appropriate in the workplace and these can and should be dealt with regardless.

Those on the autistic spectrum will benefit from suitable adjustments and should be appropriately supported at work. Narcissists, on the other hand, need serious managing, firm boundaries, to be held accountable and be made to face the consequences of their actions.

2

Why Are People Narcissistic?

You may not know much about your co-workers' personal lives (although some narcissists may enjoy telling you about themselves) but if they are a narcissist, it can be helpful for you to understand how they could have become the way they are. As we've seen, narcissism is a complex pattern of traits and behaviours with roots in early childhood experiences. It doesn't just suddenly develop overnight. As with a lot of mental health conditions and personality issues, there is an ongoing debate about nature versus nurture, so let's explore some of the main theories and understanding around this issue.

Genetics

Investigating how much of a genetic, inheritable aspect there is to narcissism is difficult and therefore studies in this area are largely limited and inconclusive. Some research suggests that there is a genetic factor to aspects of narcissism. The most relevant studies have looked at twins, who obviously share the same DNA yet have grown up in different environments. While some studies suggest a genetic link to certain traits, such as grandiosity and entitlement, it tends to be low to moderate, so, while there may be some genetic component, it doesn't seem like the strongest of explanations. Environment and life experiences are much more influential.

Generational Impact and Modelling

Narcissistic behaviour and personality traits can run in families. In my clinical work, I have seen a lot of examples of somebody with narcissistic ways of being, having grown up with a narcissistic parent. Rather than this being solely down to a biological, genetic factor though, it is typically more to do with the repeating of transgenerational cycles of behaviour and modelling.

Children learn by observing, mirroring and imitating what they see. For all of us, what we grow up with is our 'normal'. We may not consider it as anything other than that for a long time. There is powerful modelling from how we see our parents behave, how they talk to and about us, as well as how they talk to or about other people. The same is true for how we see them treat themselves and others and their thinking patterns and behaviours. Growing up with a narcissistic parent means that their own wants and needs dominate in relationships, and this is another key model of interaction that we can learn.

Narcissistic parents are inherently selfish and consumed primarily with their own thoughts, feelings, wants and needs. They are certainly not natural caregivers and so do not consistently provide the appropriate care and support children need to grow into fully functioning, considerate, caring, emotionally mature, healthy adults. They typically parent in either very neglectful, abusive or overbearing and controlling ways.

As I explain in my book *Raised by Narcissists*, being so consumed with themselves and their own emotions, narcissistic parents do not attend to the individual or emotional needs of the child, so the child does not learn how to regulate their own emotions. This can have a whole range of negative knock-on effects and implications. Children of narcissists do not tend to grow up experiencing appropriate healthy boundaries within the family, so often have a poor understanding or sense of them. They do not learn personal accountability or responsibility because, again, this has not been modelled by their narcissistic parents or family.

Children of narcissists sometimes do not learn empathy or the importance of being considerate to other people's feelings or needs, and so they take on their parents' narcissistic traits. Or there is a swing to the opposite extreme, and they go on to be highly empathic and sensitive and struggle with an overburden of guilt, responsibility or obligation. Again, there's an issue of boundaries.

While there is a generational impact, and narcissistic traits, thinking or behaviours can be modelled and learnt from one generation to the next, this does not necessarily mean a child of a narcissist will develop Narcissistic Personality Disorder. There is a big difference between narcissistic ways of being – particularly behaviour that has been learnt – and a complex personality issue. The core difference lies in what is core personality and what are learnt behaviours. Anything that has been learnt can be unlearnt.

Self-awareness and the ability to genuinely self-reflect and, importantly, experience empathy and be troubled by remorse drive a motivation to change. Change requires taking personal responsibility and action. Those who have learnt narcissistic ways of being from their family may well be able to do this. Those with a core narcissistic personality can't.

Parenting Styles

Research in this area points to two main, very distinct and extreme styles of parenting being connected to the development of narcissistic personality. These are **neglectful and abusive parenting** and **over-the-top indulgent parenting**.

In the case of significantly neglectful and abusive parenting, the child's physical, psychological and/or emotional needs are not met, in ways that lead to deep and lasting damage. It is thought that experiencing this early on in life causes a child to feel a deep sense of shame and self-loathing, extreme fear of rejection or abandonment, and in response they develop a narcissistic personality as a counter to and protection from these feelings. Narcissistic characteristics and behaviours effectively serve to keep shame well away forever more.

In narcissists higher up the NPD spectrum, this psychological damage happens so early and is so deep that they may never be able to consciously recognise it. In other words, they are trapped by their own narcissism and narcissistic thinking and they end up just believing their own self-indulgent BS.

By over-the-top, indulgent parenting, we are referring to the engulfing, overbearing parent who constantly over-praises their child without substance or merit. Constantly and inappropriately overestimating, complimenting or exaggerating a child's skill or ability can lead to an inflated and confused sense of self and ego, entitlement and identity and can lead to the development of narcissistic traits.

Sometimes adult narcissists have experienced an extreme and unpredictable combination of these two parenting styles.

Parenting styles change over time and it will be interesting to see the impacts of this in future generations. I fear that the trends of 'gentle parenting' and some parents always wanting to be liked by their child, alongside reluctance to parent with firm and fair boundaries, really won't support the understanding or learnt experience of healthy boundaries or support the development of personal accountability or responsibility. This also doesn't teach or model to children the importance of conflict resolution or emotional regulation. Parenting is difficult and nobody is going to get it right all of the time, but navigating rupture and repair in relationships is key. Encouraging social consideration and empathy is also important. These components are often found to have been distinctly lacking in the childhoods of adult narcissists.

Early and Traumatic Life Experiences

Early and traumatic life experiences play a key role in the development of Narcissistic Personality Disorder. These may include having had a neglectful and abusive parent, as described above. Or there may have been some significant disruption in their early attachment. This could be because of a parent's own issues; perhaps their own narcissism or mental health problems, addictions or illness. There may have been a sudden traumatic loss of attachment from a parent or caregivers. That can be from a sudden disruption, death, or because for some reason the child has had to leave the family home and live elsewhere.

The trauma may be from so early on in life that a person doesn't have a conscious recollection of it, but the neglect or abandonment will have been significant enough to trigger the development of narcissistic defences and narcissism.

The core basis of a narcissistic personality is considered to be formed usually within the first five years of life and certainly by the age of seven or eight. Early childhood trauma impacts on the child's ability to successfully move through early-life developmental stages, including the egocentric stage. This, it is thought, is where narcissistic adults are essentially stuck psychologically and emotionally.

If you have ever had close dealings with an adult narcissist, you may well have felt like you are dealing with an adult sized toddler trying to get their own way. That is because on some level you are.

Narcissistic traits and behaviours serve as a protective mechanism as a result of the trauma. You can understand a person's narcissistic actions as a highly effective psychological defence that protects them from ever getting in touch, getting near to, or making contact with their own feelings of shame, worthlessness, vulnerability or inadequacy. This is often in response to very early and significant childhood abuse, neglect and trauma. When an infant experiences abuse, neglect, rejection or abandonment early on in life it is too overwhelming to bear, so deep psychological defences kick in, in order that they never have to feel that way again.

As long as a person can be arrogant, dismissive, believe in their own entitlement, superiority, grandiosity, or be busy criticising, judging or shaming and blaming others, they can keep themselves away from ever getting in touch with these kinds of feelings within themselves.

Narcissism is essentially a deeply, unconscious, highly effective protective defence mechanism.

Societal Influences

Sadly, there are aspects of our modern ways of living that breed a flavour of narcissism. The Western world largely prioritises an individualistic society over collectivism or community, one in which the focus is more on individual gains and successes rather than what is good or fair for communities as a whole.

Ironically, in a world where technologically we are in some ways more connected than ever, we are simultaneously more disconnected, isolated and lonely than we've ever been.

The prevalence of social media and its influence on our society and culture, in my opinion, absolutely breeds a sense of selfishness, self-seeking and narcissism. Narcissistic people have a pathological need for attention and social media is the perfect platform for narcissists to access a quick and easy following and supply of 'likes'. This feedback can also fuel a person's addictive need for more.

Social media also places strong emphasis on the importance of looks and personal image. It fosters a competitive environment of showing off and self-promotion. There is a growth in our sense of personal entitlement and self-importance; of people believing that their experience or opinion is something that must be shared and appreciated and is of utmost importance to the rest of the world. The financial gains to be had from social media only further encourage more of this.

3

Are We Really Surrounded
by Narcissists?

This is a question I get asked a lot, along with 'Why is there so much discussion and interest in narcissists?'

Honestly, I think one of the main reasons for this is simply because there is so much of it around. Please don't panic about this! I'm not saying everyone is a narcissist, by any stretch of the imagination – true NPD accounts for a very small percentage of the population, approximately 1–6 per cent. We don't need to be hyper-vigilant for every little sign of it in all the people in our lives. However, look around and you may well recognise narcissistic behaviour across different areas of your life, at both a macro or micro level and at varying points on the spectrum. Does this mean narcissism is on the rise?

Increased Awareness

Narcissists have been around for an eternity – as we've seen, they are even captured in Greek mythology. Some studies suggest that narcissism is on the rise. We are also more informed and better at recognising it. I also believe that changing parenting styles and cultural shifts, particularly around social media and community, means there is a lot more narcissism around.

This has helped to increase awareness of *narcissistic abuse*, which can be life-changing for those who experience it. The nature of narcissistic abuse, which commonly involves gaslighting, means a person is often left feeling like they've imagined the abuse, they've misunderstood, or that it is their fault in some way. Increased awareness has helped people recognise their abuse and have their experience validated.

This has been a helpful shift and one that I've seen in my own practice over time. For many years people would come to me seeking therapy because they believed they were solely responsible for a troubled relationship. That's never the case; a relationship involves at least two people and there is always shared responsibility. (However, in the eyes of a narcissist this is never the case.) Over the years I've seen more and more people seeking help who already suspect or know they are dealing with a narcissist; this increased awareness is helpful.

The Digital Age and Social Media

As discussed in the previous chapter, social media does play a role in fuelling narcissistic behaviour as it essentially rewards self-promotion. While there are many positives to this form of communication and online community, research in this area shows that its use is positively correlated to narcissistic personality traits. The 'follows'-and-'likes' economy drives an addictive dopamine hit-driven loop that keeps people hooked. It's in the social media companies' interest to keep people on their platforms and looking at one another's posts and pictures. This also fuels constant comparison and a sense of competitiveness that can negatively impact a person's mental health, leaving people feeling low in self-esteem and at the same time fuelling perfectionist and seemingly self-centred traits.

I, like many people, have concerns that, for generations growing up in the digital age, the art of authentic, human interactions, relationship-building, empathy and conflict resolution is getting lost. Rather than learning how to effectively communicate or deal with interpersonal issues, some people have learnt how to 'block' or 'delete' instead of dealing with conflict or negative experiences in a more effective, emotionally mature way. By the nature of technologically driven cultural shifts, there has been a decrease in face-to-face social interactions and personal connection.

Economic and Cultural Factors

There are recent economic and cultural shifts that drive a much more individualistic mentality. Rising living costs mean more financial pressure for more people and this creates a fiercely competitive job market in many areas. Therefore self-serving behaviour and self-promotion at work becomes a necessity for some. There is a survival impulse at play here.

An 'everyone for themselves' way of thinking is selfish and self-serving, although not necessarily always an example of full-blown Narcissistic Personality Disorder.

Buzzwords and the Rise of the Self-Proclaimed 'Expert'

As previously noted, there are attention-supply needs to be met and financial gains to be made from sharing, and in particular, sharing about narcissism on social media – or from promoting or providing services to deal with or recover from this.

When help is offered by suitably qualified and experienced professionals, it is helpful and supportive. Importantly, too, it's often delivered in a contained, balanced manner.

Once a buzzword, narcissism, like any mental health term,

can then be followed by an overload of sharing of information and unfortunately... misinformation. We can then get into a space where the clinical meaning of narcissism gets a little lost and there is an over- or misdiagnosis from lay people in society. This is another reason why there may appear to be an increase in its prevalence that may in fact be skewed.

Not everyone who is selfish or gaslights is a narcissist – they could just be emotionally immature or defensive. As we've covered, narcissism and narcissistic personality is understood as a whole profile characterised by long-standing traits and behaviours that can be seen across different situations and relationships.

Yes, somebody may behave narcissistically sometimes. As mentioned earlier, that can be a defensive response. But it doesn't necessarily mean they are a fully fledged narcissist. For our own peace and well-being it is beneficial to have a grounded, realistic perspective; therefore I find it much more useful to describe a person's behaviour more specifically, for example, by using words like 'arrogant' or 'rude', rather than using a sweeping statement such as 'they're a narcissist'. This will also be more effective for you when discussing or reporting this kind of behaviour in the workplace. Being as specific as you can in describing the actions or behaviour of a troublesome boss or colleague is much more compelling when taking matters to HR or beyond.

The other shift that has occurred in recent years is that the area of narcissism and narcissistic abuse recovery has really taken on a whole new life of its own. Suddenly thousands of people want to share their experience and opinions across social media. It's very understandable to want to share what is such a unique and troubling experience. And narcissism and narcissistic psychology is fascinating. However, what has also emerged out of this is the rise of the self-proclaimed expert. You will see across social media platforms no end of people offering an array of posts, opinions or therapeutic services, yet, worryingly, not all of them are suitably qualified, experienced or registered to do so. Worse still, I've seen some where their given qualifications or experience are misleading or even fictitious – ironically, this is something that narcissists do!

I think, sadly, the irony sometimes is lost on some self-proclaimed narcissism 'experts' behaving in ways that are for all intents and purposes... narcissistic. I feel that this in part has encouraged a fear-based, not always well-informed, over-vigilant trend of suspecting or believing that 'everyone is a narcissist'. If you were worried, please be assured, they're not!

The Reality

While abusive behaviour is never OK and should always be named and dealt with accordingly, I think it's important to remember that not every narcissist will be abusive. They may well be irritating or difficult to work with, but they are not all necessarily going to go out of their way to cause others harm. Fortunately, we are now better supported by legislation and law to name abuse and control and to hold people accountable for it. More people are speaking out and seeking help for narcissistic abuse.

While it might seem sometimes like narcissism is everywhere, it is often more the case that we are seeing more of it due to the presence of information in the mainstream and social media.

There is more discussion and awareness of mental health issues, abuse, coercive control and specifically narcissistic abuse.

Moving Forward

When it comes to recovery from narcissistic abuse, I've always advocated for the aim of balance and the ability to be able to protect yourself. For sure, it helps to be well-informed enough to be able to recognise narcissism and narcissistic abuse and then to arm yourself with the tools to manage it as best as possible, perhaps even to work through the trauma or triggers that it so often creates. Sometimes it may be necessary to leave a job or situation because of it, to protect your own mental health and well-being. Other times it can be managed enough that you are able to live with it.

We don't always need to go running for the hills the second a narcissist is around. They are among us. You will likely come across one at work at some point in your working life. I think it is much more empowering and freeing to learn how to handle difficult people effectively and to be able to be less affected by them than trying to completely banish them from society. There have always been narcissists and there probably always will be. Learning to spot them, deal with them, to navigate tricky dynamics at work and be less affected by them is the aim. And I can assure you, that's also very possible.

4

Why Are Narcissists Successful?

Have you ever wondered why some of the most difficult people seem to reach the top? Leadership positions are frequently occupied by those with narcissistic traits – those who showcase their wealth, status and influence, often at the expense of others. The unfortunate reality is that certain narcissistic characteristics can, in fact, facilitate success, especially within specific societal, economic or corporate structures. This success frequently comes at a cost, leaving behind a legacy of harm and a community of individuals impacted by their actions – consequences to which these leaders often remain oblivious.

Understanding why this happens and recognising the signs and costs can help support your own personal awareness, so let's consider some of the components of narcissism that play a role in their apparent success.

Self-Confidence, Charm and Charisma

The first thing you'll find with overt narcissism is an unwavering self-confidence. While the rest of us may suffer from insecurities or imposter syndrome from time to time, the grandiose narcissist will strut into work like they own the place – and in many cases, they do. Healthy individuals can self-reflect and acknowledge both their strengths and their limitations. Narcissists, on the other hand, possess a striking, if not deluded, self-belief in their skills and capabilities.

I remember early on in my own career I was working with a firm of consultants when an opening arose for a team leader position that required in-depth knowledge and experience of the role and industry. Much to everyone's surprise the youngest, newest, most junior member of the team, aged nineteen with a matter of months of experience, piped up that he'd like to put himself forward for the role. I will never forget the bemused face of the manager. There was a stunned silence from everyone in the meeting. It's one thing to have ambition and confidence, but narcissists are unashamedly high in self-belief to the point of delusion. This is paired with an inability to self-reflect in a genuine way. Needless to say he didn't get the job.

Grandiose narcissists will not only say, 'I'm the best person for this job,' they will truly believe it, and their conviction is compelling. This confidence can be persuasive and magnetic at the interview stage and when presenting or networking. Many narcissists embody the notion of 'fake it till you make it' to the extreme. Narcissists naturally use their charm to win people over and – before the red flags are spotted, at least – this typically works. The confidence and charisma is enjoyable and quite something to be around and experience. However, ultimately you will find that these were the warning signs of the switch that invariably comes.

Manipulative narcissists at work know how to use the charm offensive too. They are more likely to speak up in meetings and intrinsically know what to say to who and when. This charm works especially well on people in their organisation who don't have to interact with them on a daily basis. You will see them turn the charm on and up to max when the owner, investor, big boss or external contact comes in. Upper management will see the sparkly, all-singing and -dancing charismatic version, while the rest of the workplace get the full profile.

Utterly Ruthless Pursuit of Goals

The nature of narcissistic thinking and behaviour reflects a selfish, self-seeking drive towards getting one's own wants and needs met. This is apparent across all relationships and situations, both work and professional. To reach the top often requires a single-minded focus, dogged determination and the ability to prioritise personal objectives over anything or anyone else. Narcissists are naturals at this.

Many narcissists are quite the work addicts too. Narcissists are willing to put the hours in, in pursuit of their goals of status and wealth. Power and money are important to the ego of the grandiose narcissist. In pursuit of status, material and financial success they are perfectly willing to sacrifice relationships for their own advancement, and they view people as commodities to be used for them to reach their own goals and gains. They will take credit for other people's work without any guilt or remorse. They also have the ability to make ruthless decisions that others (with empathy) would struggle with.

There are different aspects of narcissism that play a role in how heavily somebody is invested in their work. Research in the area shows a narcissistic need for admiration to be a strong predictor of global and personal meaning of and engagement in work. The need for admiration often drives narcissistic leaders in work, in business, in global politics, religion or the health industry. Narcissistic rivalry is a strong predictor of work addiction and family/work conflict. Their competitiveness and need to be better than others drive narcissists at work.

Political Skill

Political skill is basically being able to understand and influence others in order to achieve personal or professional objectives. It's the ability to navigate people at work, relationships, social situations and power dynamics to essentially get things done in the way you want. A 2025 study highlighted 'political skill' as the critical moderating factor in the narcissist's success in the workplace. Grandiose, overt narcissists with high political skill achieve higher workplace status, success and satisfaction.

My colleague Andrew had an uncanny ability to present himself perfectly in every dynamic. In meetings, he'd nod in all the right places and agree to all the opposing views. Afterwards, he'd approach each person privately and get in their ear to say he completely understood and how he was onside with their views and ideas. People believed him to be their biggest ally. But he would do this with everyone. Then he'd tell the director how he was the only reasonable voice in the team and how he was the best-placed person to bridge the divide between the others. Nobody was surprised when he got promoted – he'd orchestrated the whole thing to get what he wanted.

Narcissistic Leadership

Many narcissists, especially the overt kind, are natural leaders. They are charismatic and able to inspire and motivate others through their confidence and pioneering vision. They are persuasive and can visualise and paint compelling pictures of success. They are also not shy of the limelight and being the centre of attention. Their confidence and self-belief mean they are comfortable making bold decisions quickly. They are determined.

One study looked at narcissism in the hospitality industry. This sector is well known for its high energy and people-focused nature. It highlighted the double-sided influence of narcissistic leadership; on the one hand, they can help amplify the unheard voices of the employees, encouraging or even forcing staff to speak up, yet at the same time they can fuel workplace conflict by generating toxic interactions and workplace bullying. This is basically like having a manager who is simultaneously your biggest cheerleader and champion, and your worst nightmare and bully, depending on the time of day. Many people describe their narcissistic boss as a Jekyll and Hyde character.

You find narcissists at work as either leaders or lone wolves – they are not team players. They prefer a power dynamic where they can reign over others, rather than a flat, transparent or equal hierarchy.

Sales and Networking

Narcissists are networking ninjas – they are inherently skilled at reading people, charming and telling people what they want to hear. They excel at making powerful first impressions and identifying who can offer them something they want. Once they recognise a contact that can be useful to them, they will remember everyone's name, their spouse's name, their dog's name, all their interests, their favourite hobbies and food, all their likes and dislikes and so on... not because they care, but because information is power and power is a favourite tool. This is what helps them to be successful salespeople.

Manipulative narcissists also present and position themselves as indispensable. They can become quite the chameleon in terms of adapting their persona to different audiences. It can be quite alarming to witness. I've literally seen people completely change personality between being in and out of meetings at work.

Emotional Management

Narcissists use emotions to manipulate. Narcissist rage, anger and aggression is used to intimidate and bully others and control the workforce. Their emotions can appear volatile. However, when needed they can also be managed, to striking levels. Some narcissists are so disconnected they appear to not experience anxiety, so they are fearless and bold. When this is paired with confidence and self-belief they use it to drive their success. They are often calm in a crisis or among chaos.

Narcissists tend not to be rattled by drama or conflict – in fact they thrive on it.

They relish being in a position of power and so will do anything to maintain or extend that. They have a need to dominate and want others to fear them.

As we've seen, too, narcissists do not experience empathy in the same way as non-narcissistic people, so they don't feel remorse in the way that others do. This also plays a role in enabling them to charge forward with their plans and goals regardless of the impact on anyone else. In other words, they don't care who gets harmed in their single-minded pursuit of success. They're the kind that would 'sell their own grandmother'!

Narcissists are master performers and, while they don't experience emotions in the same way most non-narcissistic people do, intelligent narcissists are highly skilled at understanding emotions on a cognitive level. This means they can learn how to come across like a caring colleague or boss, or even friend – however, again, as always, their motives come back down to their own selfish agenda.

Manipulative and Exploitative

Ultimately one of the key clinical characteristics of the narcissistic personality is being highly manipulative and exploitative of other people. So narcissists are innately attuned to what's important to other people and use this to really sell a job, product or concept to others. They are great at telling people what they think they want to hear. This occurs all the way through the employment process, starting from the interview stage, as well as being a part of how they are in the role and how they interact with colleagues or clients.

With skill and flair, they identify your core values and goals in life or work. They then use what they know matters most to you in order to manipulate and exploit you for their own benefit. They don't really care about you ever getting what or to where you want to be. Their own goals and success are all that matter to them.

Narcissistic people in sales promise the world to customers and are shameless in their assurances and guarantees. They will then back out of the way and let colleagues deal with any fallout or issues, denying any wrongdoing – because for narcissistic bosses and colleagues, any problems or failures are *always* somebody else's fault. They will never take personal responsibility. For this same reason, narcissists in the workplace won't take on board any feedback or criticism. Many react badly to these and subsequently punish those who dare to suggest anything that doesn't support their fantasy of their own self-importance or ability. We will look more at the ways they punish shortly.

They like to keep you latched on to believing your professional hopes and dreams will be met if you just stick by them. It rarely happens though. Being grounded in reality around narcissistic bosses and colleagues is particularly important.

Why Narcissistic Success Is Unsustainable

While narcissists may achieve 'success', it is often relatively short-term or limited. It more often than not ultimately comes crashing down at some point.

Charlie joined a marketing agency as a senior account manager. Charismatic and confident, she quickly impressed leadership with polished presentations and bold ideas.

She presented her team's work as her own vision, using 'I' rather than 'we' in presentations. When campaigns succeeded, Charlie took centre stage. When they failed, she blamed team members or clients. Her confidence was magnetic. Clients loved her assurance. The board saw her as the future – dynamic, ambitious and results-driven. Within eighteen months, Charlie was promoted to creative director – the youngest person to hold the position in the company's history.

As CD, Charlie could no longer rely on others' work to prop up her image. The role required strategic thinking, genuine leadership and the ability to develop talent – skills she did not possess.

She pitched an ambitious rebrand without consulting her senior team. The strategy was flashy but flawed. When colleagues raised concerns, she dismissed them publicly as difficult and 'resistant to change'.

Within six months of her promotion, three senior creatives resigned. Exit interviews revealed credit-stealing, public humiliation and impossible demand. Without her talented team, campaign results declined. When a major client threatened to leave, Charlie blamed the account team – the client left anyway. It started to become increasingly apparent that Charlie's reports were heavy on spin, light on substance. When challenged on declining revenue, she became defensive and accusatory. She had surrounded herself with junior staff who wouldn't challenge her, alienating the experienced colleagues she needed most.

A year later the agency posted its first annual loss in a decade. Staff morale was catastrophically low. The board asked Charlie to step down. Charlie left blaming everyone but herself – the board, her team, market conditions. She never, ever acknowledged her part in the decline.

Charlie rose quickly because narcissistic traits – confidence, charisma, self-promotion – can look like leadership in the short term. But sustainable success requires empathy, collaboration and genuine competence. Narcissists can climb the ladder by standing on others' shoulders, but they can't stay there because, eventually, there's no one left to exploit and nowhere left to hide their inadequacies. And usually, the higher the position, the more visible the flaws.

Narcissists at work typically burn bridges with colleagues and partners. They create toxic work environments and as a result generate high turnover of staff and may be faced with the results or consequences of that and/or other actions. Narcissistic people struggle to maintain long-term relationships of any kind, including professional relationships and so eventually it all breaks down. People start to wise up to their manipulation and abuse and so distance and protect themselves. True innovation and professional success usually require genuine collaboration and teamwork.

Successful businesses or organisations take into consideration diverse perspectives and give space to individual ideas. They work together in a collaborative and supportive manner.

They also engage in sustainable and ethical practices and encourage a culture of learning and growth, where staff can learn from mistakes and use them to shape things in a positive, productive way. Narcissists struggle with all of this, which means they will typically only attain a superficial success – one that lacks depth or longevity.

There is a predictable pattern of narcissistic success.

First, there is the initial rise, fuelled by a drive to gain material wealth, markers of superficial success, connections and positions of power and status. Then there is a period of peak performance. This is driven by ego and ambition and may last for some time. However, then follows a gradual decline. Relationships deteriorate, reputations are hampered and, frankly, they just can no longer get away with what they once did, in the way they once did it. Then comes the eventual fall and crash, when competence can no longer match promises or the people around them are no longer willing to play ball. They are ousted or held accountable for their abusive or destructive actions.

This dynamic only needs to start to turn and most narcissists in the workplace will swiftly move on to elsewhere – just like Narcissus from Greek mythology, they will continue in their hunt for the attention and affections of someone and something else, but are never truly satisfied. Once they know they've been rumbled they rarely hang around to have their true selves be seen. They will, though, typically exit in a way that leaves them with a sense of having won. Either they sell out or reach some kind of financial settlement, or there is some kind of battle won that they could frame in whichever way serves them to feel like it was on their terms. Ultimately though, they move on.

The Drive to Succeed

You can see that a fundamental part of grandiose narcissism is an intrinsic desire for 'success'. Because narcissists place the highest value on superficial qualities – such as appearance, material possessions, status and financial success – they are fundamentally driven to pursue and acquire these things above all else. Their lack of empathy means they also do not care who or what they harm in their pursuit of success. Power and status are highly important to them, and this is yet another reason why they *need* to attain certain professional positions. Wherever there are dynamics of power or status, you will find narcissists. I'm not saying every single time, but you will find a higher percentage of them in positions of power or status, to any degree.

Seeing this is understandably frustrating and worrying. Particularly if you've experienced all the trouble that comes with working for or with somebody like this. If it's any saving grace at all though, please know that narcissistic 'success' is superficial, unfulfilling and unsustainable. A part of the pathology of narcissistic personality is a deep-seated discontentment. Nothing is ever enough or good enough for a narcissist. Many grandiose narcissists are driven in a compulsive, addict-like way to seek more and more and more, or something new, or something 'better'. This is driven by deep-seated discontent and dissatisfaction. The latest 'success', material purchase, holiday, partner or achievement merely serves as a temporary fix to feel enough. Material wealth and possessions, and even people, are used so the narcissist can appear and look, and even feel, superior and successful. But it's not lasting or sustainable. Also, let's face it, superficial 'success' can only get a person so far.

Authentic Success

This isn't about condemning ambition or confidence at all. There is a vast difference between healthy drive and destructive self-interest. Authentic, sustainable success comes from:

- Competence and skill, backed by genuine hard work and development.
- Confidence – that is rooted in realistic self-reflection and assessment, not delusion.
- Leadership that elevates and supports others, not just selfish or self-promotion.
- Achievement that creates value for all involved.

An ideal goal is to create systems that reward authentic success over narcissistic manipulation. When we understand the mechanisms behind narcissistic success, we can make more informed decisions about who we follow, who we support or promote and what kind of success we want to be around or achieve for ourselves.

Remember that, while narcissists may 'win' in the shorter term, sustainable true success – both personal and professional – comes from building value, cultivating authentic relationships and creating positive impact that extends beyond one's own selfish goals.

Reflections

Of course, it can be extremely frustrating and upsetting to see an abusive narcissist do well off the back of cheating, lying, manipulation or exploitation. I also believe though that it is worthwhile to consider and remind yourself of your own definition of 'success'. For example, I have experienced narcissistic people plagiarising my work, and it is very difficult to see somebody unashamedly profit from this theft and deception. However, I ask myself – how genuinely fulfilling can it be to claim success from these kinds of endeavours? Can the narcissist really feel good about that? Are they truly happy? No. Narcissists are deeply troubled, dissatisfied, discontented people and nothing they do, or have, will ever truly give them genuine peace, fulfilment or happiness. I think it can be helpful to remind yourself of that when faced with seeing a narcissist 'thrive', and to return the focus to what matters most to you in your life. Stay focused on your own moral compass and values and remind yourself that you can have more of what brings you more important meaning in life; like connection, contentment and integrity.

Success reflects our values and what really matters to us in ourselves, our lives and the world. Narcissistic people who are wealthy or in positions of power don't necessarily have lasting, meaningful success. It might look like it on the outside, because of course image and projection matters, but behind the scenes, behind closed doors, it's not.

5

Which Professions Attract Narcissists?

Wherever there is power, status or wealth there will be narcissists. And wherever there are narcissists there is chaos, drama and abuse.

So, with *power, status or wealth* as a working definition, obvious career magnets for narcissists include:

- Politics
- Entertainment
- Social media influencing
- Academia/teaching
- Law
- Medical sector
- Alternative health/well-being
- Charity sector

I'll explain more about the attraction for narcissists within each sector, as well as how certain sectors attract a specific type of narcissist. But first, let's look at the main sub-types.

The Three Sub-Types of Narcissist at Work

In any sector, you will come across one of three main kinds of narcissist at work: *agentic, antagonistic* and *communal* narcissists.

Agentic Narcissists

Agentic narcissists are characterised by an individual sense of self-importance, dominance and achievement that often drives power, success and admiration. They pursue self-promotion and grandiosity and are therefore typically arrogant, assertive and dominant.

Agentic narcissists at work tend to:

Make self-promoting statements: 'I single-handedly turned that project around' or 'The client specifically asked for me to lead this'.

Exaggerate achievements: 'I increased revenue by 40 per cent' (when it was a team effort) or 'I've never failed to meet a target'.

Use competitive positioning: 'I'm the only one here with the experience to handle this' or 'No one else could have closed that deal'.

Display future grandiosity: 'I'll be running this company within five years'.

Dismiss others' contributions: 'That's helpful, however, let me show you how it's really done' or 'Good effort, but I'll take it from here'.

They also name-drop, take credit for other people's work, talk over others and exploit others for their own gain.

Agentic narcissists are relentlessly focused on climbing the ladder. Every interaction, project and relationship is evaluated through the lens of 'How does this advance my career?' They're skilled at making themselves look indispensable while making others feel dispensable. Unlike antagonistic narcissists, who are openly hostile, agentic narcissists may appear charming and competent – especially to those in power – while systematically using colleagues as rungs on their ladder to success.

Antagonistic Narcissists

Antagonistic narcissists at work are driven by self-protective motives – they seek to defend themselves from any possible or perceived threat, they are highly defensive and aggressive and will protect themselves by devaluing others.

Antagonistic narcissists will:

Publicly criticise and put others down: 'Did you actually think that through before speaking?'

Be highly dismissive: 'That's basic – nothing impressive'.

Use competitive comparisons: 'When I was at your level, I was already managing twice your workload'.

Use threats and intimidation: 'If you can't handle this, I'll find someone who can' or 'This mistake could cost you your career here'.

Be sarcastic and undermining: 'Well, that's one way to do it – the wrong way'.

They are confrontational, will blame and shame others to make themselves feel superior, and they will deliberately sabotage at work.

Antagonistic narcissists create an atmosphere of constant tension where colleagues live in fear and walk on eggshells. Their behaviour is designed to keep others off-balance, insecure and submissive. Unlike other narcissistic types, who may charm initially, antagonistic narcissists often show their hostility early – they simply don't care about being liked as long as they're dominant.

Communal Narcissists

Communal narcissists seek gains from their contrived efforts to appear altruistic and admirable from within community settings and sectors. They attempt to appear kind, trustworthy and caring – but ultimately seek to be part of the elite.

Communal narcissists at work display:

Performative caring: 'I'm always here for the team – I put everyone else's needs before my own' or 'I care more about people than profits'.

Martyr status: 'I stayed until midnight helping Sarah with her project' or 'I've sacrificed so much for this team'.

Moral superiority: 'Unlike some people, I actually care about making a difference' or 'I'm driven by purpose, not personal gain'.

Humble-bragging: 'People say I'm just too generous with my time'.

Saviour language: 'They really needed me to step in' or 'I don't know what this team would do without me'.

They will also make public displays of helpfulness (in front of the right people at work), and will violate your boundaries through the guise of 'care', or triangulate through 'concern'.

Communal narcissists are typically covert and seek admiration through appearing exceptionally caring, selfless or morally superior. They want to be seen as the most dedicated, the most values-driven person in the room. However, their 'generosity' always comes with strings attached – they're keeping score and expect recognition, gratitude and loyalty in return.

The Communal Narcissism Inventory, devised in 2012, is a psychological measure designed to capture scores to the following statements, which highlight the specific kind of narcissism you will find in many sectors and industries. The statements are:

- I am the most helpful person I know.
- I am going to bring peace and justice to the world.
- I am the best friend someone can have.
- I will be well known for the good deeds I will have done.
- I am (going to be) the best parent on this planet.
- I am the most caring person in my social surrounding.
- In the future, I will be well known for solving the world's problems.
- I greatly enrich others' lives.
- I will bring freedom to the people.
- I am an amazing listener.
- I will be able to solve world poverty.

- I have a very positive influence on others.
- I am generally the most understanding person.
- I'll make the world a much more beautiful place.
- I am extraordinarily trustworthy.
- I will be famous for increasing people's well-being.

You can see how, on the face of this, some of these aspirations appear quite admirable. However, their importance and sense of grandiosity is what distinguishes them as a flavour of communal narcissism. Of course, many of us want to strive to achieve, or do our best, or make a positive impact. But for narcissists this is extreme and the pursuit often ruthless. The core aim is actually selfish notoriety, status and power, not altruism or generosity, for the good of the people. You can see how the statements fit with the kinds of sectors we're discussing, including politics, health and well-being, medical, the charity sector, academia and law.

The Professions

Politics

Being a political leader brings ultimate power. Agentic narcissists are highly motivated by control and leadership and have the capacity to enforce aggressive or 'tough' political policies. The world of politics is like a playground for anyone who genuinely believes they can solve everyone's problems while simultaneously believing that everyone else is doing it wrong. Some politicians are basically professional narcissists with campaign budgets, spending their days telling crowds how wonderful they are and somehow managing to make a national crisis become an opportunity to promote their personal brand. Being in a position of political power feeds the ego and provides the narcissist with the attention and adoration they pathologically need. Even negative attention is attention. Having major world decisions, including war, within one's reach and control is of course ultimate global power. Being a politician is also one of the only jobs you can be bad, or even completely fail at, and still get a book deal at the end of it.

Arguably, an element of agentic and communal narcissism is needed for someone to be bold enough to want to be a political leader. Power dynamics are rife. For the non-narcissistic well-intentioned, although it clearly can be done, working in politics is certainly not for the faint-hearted.

Hollywood and the Entertainment Industry

Similarly, Hollywood and the entertainment industry serve as natural habitat for narcissists. Actors and performers spend their careers pretending to be other people – perfect for someone already pretending to be something they're not or for those who believe they are more important than they are, or nicer than they are. It's the perfect playing ground for narcissistic supply. Narcissistic celebrities are heavily indulged in 'look at me' and the focus and attention being on them. Again, it's a largely superficial and cut-throat industry, with a strong focus on looks and image. Not everyone in Hollywood will be a narcissist but, again, you'd probably need to naturally have a strong inclination for attention and fame to be able to deal with it.

Social Media and Influencing

A modern career that is perfect for agentic and communal narcissists is social media. This is a job that simply didn't exist until fairly recently, but is also a dream job for self-proclaimed experts and influencers. It's a dangerously self-perpetuating phenomenon, largely due to the monetisation of posts and likes. Social media is an alarmingly quick and easy way for a narcissist to seek out and receive the narcissistic supply they need to be able to function. The number of likes or followers becomes crucial to hold up the fragile ego of the narcissist. While the social media influencer gains all that they need, in terms of attention, financial gains and status, and portraying or displaying a 'wonderful' life, this can negatively impact other people's self-esteem and self-worth. Being bombarded with messages about how 'perfect' the narcissistic social media influencer's life appears to be, or how much they earn, or how much you might need whatever product or service they shamelessly flog, will only ever leave a person feeling low or less than. Fortunately, it's an area of narcissism that is relatively easily avoided if you use social media with caution and limitations.

Academia

The world of academia is full of the brightest minds and some of the kindest, most generous and well-meaning, caring people. It is also rife with narcissism. For many narcissists and all sub-types seeking power, there is a ready-made dynamic of professor-over-student in academic settings. There is recognition to be had for intellectual achievements, research or publications. Lectures can become performances with a captive audience. A narcissistic professor or teacher can easily surround themselves with admiring, ambitious students who will give them narcissistic supply. Some may be vulnerable to being manipulated or abused – the difference in the power dynamic plays a key role in that. Bullying and toxic competition can become a part of the culture among colleagues in many universities and academic settings.

Dr Helena's office wall told the story she wanted everyone to see: framed journal covers, conference keynote certificates, a photo with a Nobel laureate. At forty-two, she was the university's youngest full professor and director of its Centre for Cognitive Research.

'My latest paper just got accepted,' she announced at the lab meeting, sliding copies across the table. Her three PhD students exchanged glances. They recognised the data – it was her student Gail's work from her thesis chapter.

'Congratulations,' Gail said carefully. 'I see you're first author.'

'Well, it's my lab, my funding, my research direction,' Helena replied smoothly. 'Your name is there – third author. That's generous for a student contribution.'

Gail had designed the study, collected the data and written the first draft. But she said nothing. Helena controlled her references, her future job prospects, her entire career trajectory.

Later, in the departmental kitchen, Gail found Tom, a postdoc who'd left Helena's lab the previous year.

'She presented my work at three conferences,' Tom said quietly, 'each time as her own breakthrough. When I published without adding her name – on research she never touched – she blocked my contract renewal.'

'Can't we report this?' Gail asked.

Tom shook his head. 'It's all within the grey areas. "Standard practice". "Lab conventions". She's too clever to cross clear lines.'

Six months later, Gail left the programme. So did another student. Then another.

The university investigated. Nothing formal was proven, but whispers spread through the academic community. Conference invitations stopped coming. Talented researchers chose other labs.

Helena still had her title, her office, her wall of achievements. But her empire – built on others' work – was crumbling. In academia, she'd learnt too late, reputation is everything. And hers was finally catching up with her.

Law

The legal profession offers a stage for even more sophisticated narcissistic performances. It is particularly attractive to antagonistic narcissists. It's a place where you can legitimately be argumentative, have a sense of self-righteousness and a strong sense of importance, and seek to devalue and bring others down. Lawyers essentially get paid to stand up in front of rooms full of people and perform while explaining why the other party is wrong. Law is a profession that attracts well-intentioned, well-meaning people and, like politics, it's not a career for the faint-hearted, due to the prevalence of antagonistic narcissism, power dynamics and fierce competitiveness.

Medicine and Healthcare

Medicine and healthcare are also professions that attract well-meaning caring people; however, at the same time, due to the positions of power offered in the medical and healthcare world, they also attract personalities that seek out and thrive off that. Medical and healthcare fields provide positions of power and power dynamics such as doctors or psychiatrists, where the narcissist can be in a role of authority and seniority, have control and be the all-knowing, all-powerful, arrogant person others look up to. Sadly, many narcissists will abuse that power, and this is often where you will see medical gaslighting, bullying, manipulation and exploitation.

The Charity Sector

The charity sector is also one full of the loveliest, most hard-working, well-intentioned people you could ever wish to meet, many seeking to make positive, lasting contributions in their work. Unfortunately, however, charity work also appeals to a certain kind of communal narcissist, who wants to dine out on their displays of apparent altruism and seek admiration, control and power over others. Here you can also find agentic and antagonistic narcissism in the form of self-promoting, arrogant or aggressive workers.

Corporate Leadership

Corporate leadership roles are also attractive to narcissists. They come with impressive titles, their own office, a captive audience of people who must listen to the narcissist, and people in these roles have the power to make or influence important decisions.

'I don't know what this team would do without Rachel,' the manager said during the quarterly review.

Rachel smiled humbly. 'I just care about people. It's who I am.'

Around the table, three colleagues exchanged glances. They knew better.

When James joined the team, Rachel was first to welcome him. She mentored him, stayed late reviewing his work, introduced him to 'important people'. He felt genuinely grateful – until he disagreed with her in a meeting.

The warmth vanished overnight. Rachel stopped answering his questions. Then she began sharing her 'concerns' about him with the team lead.

'I'm just worried about James,' she said, voice heavy with false concern. 'After everything I've done to support him, he seems... struggling. Ungrateful, really.'

Rachel had positioned herself as the team's emotional centre – the one everyone confided in. But information shared in confidence had a way of spreading, always prefaced with 'I'm only telling you because I care...'

When the company launched a diversity initiative, Rachel volunteered immediately and constantly posted about it on LinkedIn. But when a junior colleague privately asked for advice about discrimination, Rachel was suddenly unavailable. No witnesses meant no credit.

Rachel's kindness was transactional. Her support was conditional on loyalty and public gratitude.

She didn't want to help people. She wanted to be worshipped for it.

And anyone who failed to pay tribute learnt quickly – Rachel's warmth could turn ice-cold.

Grandiose, overt narcissists tend to be drawn to the most obvious positions of power. Covert narcissists will also be found in the workplace, in slightly more subtle positions of power or status, like within the health or well-being space, or in more supportive roles. They can also be the colleague who seeks to get their attention needs met by constantly gossiping or discussing problems and thus pulling people into listener, counsellor, carer type roles. You can learn to spot more of this by understanding 'the drama triangle' that I'll explain more about shortly.

None of these professions are bad! They are all wonderful areas of work and provide brilliant careers, and of course not everyone in them is narcissistic. However, generally speaking, anywhere where there are positions of power, status or wealth there will be all three sub-types of narcissist seeking gains, supply and success over others. Additionally, wherever there are narcissists there will be manipulation and exploitation. There will also be enablers working hard to support and protect them. The key is learning how to spot this in individuals and organisations, and discerning who has genuine, right intentions, and who is just good at making others think they do.

6

Can Narcissists Change?

This is a question I get asked a lot. Can narcissists change? Do they change? Will they change?

I think this question often reflects the hopes and well-wishes of the person asking the question. Good people want to see the best in others and believe they *can* change. Or like to think or hope they'd *want* to.

However, in short, when it comes to Narcissistic Personality Disorder the answer is 'probably not'. I'll explain why...

Psychologically, behavioural change relies on two key components: awareness and motivation.

Before we can change anything we need to firstly be aware that there is a problem. This is the first major hurdle for anyone with Narcissistic Personality Disorder. Part of narcissistic psychology is distorted thinking and lacking any real, genuine or meaningful self-awareness or insight. Narcissists struggle to self-reflect. It's very hard, if not impossible, for very narcissistic people to consider their own actions or the impact of them on anybody else. The narcissistic mind simply and immediately concludes that any difficulty of any kind is always somebody else's fault – and therefore somebody else's problem to address. It's like a short circuit in the mind; they cannot consider themselves or their own actions as being an issue. An immediate defence to feeling shame is to blame, so the narcissistic mind will immediately point fingers.

Without the ability to a) have awareness that there is a problem and b) consider the part they may have to play in that, it's very difficult to even recognise any need for change.

The other requirement for behavioural change is motivation. Usually something needs to be painful or bad enough to want to change. When people look to action behavioural change, like quitting smoking, losing weight or making some other kind of positive change, it's fundamental that the change is preferable to staying as is and continuing to experience the current discomfort and negative effects, or just waiting until it gets worse. At some point, the present becomes painful enough to motivate, drive and propel somebody towards change.

For example, you may have picked up this book because a part of your current situation has become troublesome enough to a) make you aware that there is a problem that is negatively impacting you, and b) motivate you to take some steps to change, such as learning more about narcissism in the workplace and developing some insights and coping strategies. This is change in action.

A person on the lower end of the spectrum of narcissism, who is able to hold meaningful insight and awareness about themselves and be emotionally and morally impacted enough to sustain motivation to change, is capable of working towards change. Most narcissists from the mid-range of the spectrum and above aren't and can't.

A true narcissist is unable to self-reflect objectively and realistically enough to recognise any need for change within themselves. They do not consider or really see the impact of their actions on anyone else, and, even if they could, they do not experience enough emotional empathy to care. Simply put, they don't and won't feel bad enough or responsible enough to ever truly be motivated to change. Instead, their typical unchangeable position is that either problems or improvements do not exist (denial) or that any issue is somebody else's fault (blame) and therefore for everyone else to sort out (lack of responsibility).

Interestingly, sometimes you might see a narcissist look like they are working on themselves or seeking to change. However, if you spot a pattern of lots of well-placed talk going on about it, without much action, that is more than likely a sign of 'manipulation and hook'. It's designed to serve a function, not for change but for manipulating others. Some people will talk all about what they plan to do, what they will do or what they could do, without ever really taking the steps to work on themselves and change. Change is an action, not just words.

Can narcissists change? No. At best they will dangle a carrot of hope about change in order to maintain and continue to keep people invested or close to them and to control and exploit others. Trying to get a narcissist to change, or waiting for them to change, or living in hope that they will change one day, is futile and will only take a further toll on you.

What you can change is how you respond and deal with them – and learning how to do so is entirely empowering and freeing.

Narcissists in Therapy

Typically, the unwavering perspective of most overt narcissists is 'it's YOU and YOUR fault'. Not them, ever. And as we've seen, for those with NPD the insight and motivation are just not there. So as far as they're concerned, you and everyone else are the ones with the problem and the ones who need and should go to therapy.

That said, sometimes the more covert kinds of narcissist will attend therapy or workplace coaching or mentoring. However, this is rarely with humility or the kind of engagement most people arrive with. Covert narcissists are more willing than the grandiose kinds to share signs of 'vulnerability' in order to get their needs met. This includes saying they are struggling or need help. Covert narcissists tend to position themselves as perpetual victims, claiming they have been wronged or are hard done by.

As with most things narcissists do, if they do attend counselling it is usually as a means to serve their own needs. In other words, they go because it gives them some kind of leverage.

In my line of work as a counselling psychologist, I would say I've only seen a handful of people with what I would consider fully fledged grandiose narcissism, in other words who are high on the spectrum. I have seen many more covert, vulnerable narcissists. The first time, I was not so informed or prepared to recognise it, but the dynamic is unique from the start. You can definitely learn a lot from spotting covert, vulnerable narcissism.

There is, in my experience, a very particular flavour when a narcissist arrives to therapy or coaching. First of all, they have already tried to push boundaries before we've even started – such as requesting some kind of special treatment, like a reduced rate or an alternative out-of-hours time to meet. Usually, to start with they are on the charm offensive. Compliments and favourable comparisons galore. It's very easy to be seduced by this, if you are not adequately experienced, informed or prepared. You'll hear things like 'you're the best', 'nobody has ever understood me like you do', or 'nobody has ever had the intelligence, skill or ability to', and so on. You may hear stories about a long line of previous therapists they've seen who failed in one way or another or have caused them harm. Some of what they say may indeed be the case – but some may not. When you're better-informed about narcissism, you can learn to see the charm and victimhood more as the red flag that it is. Narcissists are skilful at making a person feel amazing, special and 'chosen'.

Narcissists usually have very unrealistic expectations. So, in therapy or coaching they may expect you to know and understand them after one session, and look for you to magically fix things in an instant. By the way, they won't be prepared or willing to do any of the work – it's all on the therapist, counsellor or coach.

In other work environments, too, they will have similarly wild expectations of you and others, and no regard or consideration as to what you might need to do to meet their impossible-to-please demands.

In a therapeutic situation, it soon becomes apparent that the narcissist is not genuinely interested in changing or working on themselves and that, instead, they prefer to maintain an issue that invites sympathy or a captive audience to listen to. You may recognise this in colleagues who want to share or complain about some problem or frustration yet never really take any steps to action any positive change or resolution. The more covert type of narcissist gains from being a perpetual victim. So there becomes a function for them in having ongoing gripes or issues as that serves to gain them sympathy or support and ultimately the kind of attention they need.

The overly confident narcissist may arrogantly tell the coach, trainer or therapist all about what they already know or have accomplished.

A power dynamic and struggle inevitably ensue. The narcissist needs to control the process in relationships and situations. They will aim to do this in any way they can. This can include being evasive or aggressive or appearing vulnerable in order to manipulate or control the conversation or process. This is also a way to appear as if they are engaging in therapy; however, they can quite skilfully navigate this so that they end up being quite therapy-avoidant. Being able to claim 'I go to therapy' can also be used as a tactic to show other people they are willing or able to do the work, in a martyr-like manner, or they may guilt-trip others over the fact that they themselves are not in therapy.

Ultimately though, as we've seen, the motivation, willingness to accept accountability and engagement is actually not there, or if it is it cannot be sustained. It can be faked initially, but even narcissists can only pretend for so long.

Because of their need to be in control in relationships, therapy or coaching usually ends when they say so. It's often abrupt. Narcissists don't manage endings well – in any context. As in the workplace, the intervention invariably has not worked or has not been 'good enough', and in the eyes of the narcissist it's entirely the therapist/coach/trainer's fault. Any lack of success is due to the inadequacies of the other person. When a narcissist no longer receives enough 'supply' – that is attention, admiration or awe – from a person, they tend to blame, shame or punish them and move on. They possess a pathological need to seek these things from people and so must go and find it from wherever and whoever they can. And so the narcissistic process and dynamic continues.

PART TWO:
NARCISSISM AT WORK

7

Are You Working with a Narcissist?

We've covered understanding what narcissism is and the origins and prevalence of it. Now, let's focus in on the main defining characteristics and behaviours of clinical narcissism and how it may present specifically in the workplace. If you are having trouble with someone at work and suspect they may be a narcissist, ask yourself whether any of the following core behaviours are familiar, and, if so, to what degree.

Grandiose Sense of Self-Importance

Fundamentally, narcissistic people believe they are better than and superior to others. They believe they know more and have achieved more than everyone else. It's important for them to take this stance. They will brag and boast about themselves and simultaneously undermine, criticise and put down other people. Basically, when others feel bad, the narcissist feels better about themselves. Narcissists in the workplace have an overinflated sense of their own importance and value, believing that they do so much. They will over-embellish their involvement and contribution to successes and happily take credit for other people's work, yet if any issues arise they will take no responsibility whatsoever and will instead quickly blame and shame everyone else. Narcissists are certainly not team players!

Robert joined the team and in the first marketing meeting declared, 'I single-handedly transformed three global companies... I've been told by them all I'm the best guy for transformation they've ever seen.' He took full credit for the success of those companies and went on to dismiss other campaign strategies as 'amateur'. He put up a huge portrait of himself behind his desk so it would 'inspire creativity', and he insisted on being called 'The Visionary' rather than his actual job title of marketing director. When praise came for the team's work, he was the first to step forward to state that they were all his own ideas and that he'd run the entire project himself, with others in the team merely doing the basic tasks or 'doing the coffee run'. This created such huge issues within the team that two members of staff resigned shortly afterwards.

The most grandiose type of narcissists at work arrive with stories about their own lives, their careers, special abilities, skills and unique achievements. How much truth there is to this is always debatable. It creates a massive amount of disharmony in the team if it is not managed, though.

Need for Admiration

In any context or role, narcissists need more or less constant admiration and attention from others. A pathological need for admiration is one of the reasons why you will find narcissistic leaders in roles or industries where they can be positioned as an expert or 'guru', or where they can find a captive audience of followers. The world of celebrity is one area where this need for a fan club, literally, can easily be met. As is being an online influencer or amassing a following where an admiration 'fix' can be quickly and consistently met with engagement of this kind. Business professions and the medical and healthcare sectors often offer the kinds of roles and positions that supply this, as do law, the charity sector and even the spiritual well-being arena.

I remember going to one yoga class many years ago; however it wasn't so much a class, as nothing was being taught. Instead it was more of an 'audience with' said yoga instructor. The 'class' basically served as a captive audience for the teacher to perform and show off her own bendy abilities without any guidance or opportunity for anybody else to try or learn. In fact, it essentially consisted of a group of bemused attendees watching a performance we hadn't really signed up for. One lady got up and left, much to the annoyance of the teacher, who aggressively shouted out after her. Needless to say, I (and probably most people there that day) never returned.

In the workplace, narcissists need attention and admiration all the time. They will boast about their successes, deals, achievements – whether real or imagined. They will take credit for all that they can, regardless of their input, so they receive the praise and accolade.

Lack of Empathy

As previously outlined, a lack of ability to experience genuine empathy is a key characteristic of narcissism and narcissistic psychology. Simply put, narcissistic bosses and colleagues do not really care about anybody but themselves. They have little or no authentic compassion. Narcissists do not experience empathy in the same way other people do. If a kind of 'learnt' empathy is expressed by a narcissist in the workplace, it may be as a means for them to manipulate people to get what they want. The more covert types of narcissists are willing to appear caring; however, you will find in time that there is no real substance to it, it *feels* phoney or insincere; and ultimately time will tell if a person's words and actions align.

A narcissistic boss or colleague won't register if you're struggling with workload, stress or burnout or are troubled by personal issues in your life. It simply won't register with them that you're tired, stressed or sick. It's not realistic to expect any genuine care, understanding or sympathy from them. They are more likely to respond to the needs or emotions of others with irritability or aggression. They won't think twice about calling you when you're off sick or on holiday. They work like robots (which is really not healthy) and expect others to be the same.

Managing and attending to your own work-related self-care needs is really going to be down to you, because a narcissistic boss or manager would happily keep you working until you drop – and then simply replace you with the next person. Your self-care is your responsibility and having the boundaries to manage this in difficult work environments is key. Boundaries are vitally important in working with narcissistic types and we'll go into this in more detail later.

Preoccupied with 'Success'

One of the defining clinical characteristics of Narcissistic Personality Disorder is a preoccupation with ideas and fantasies of success, power, or their own brilliance, beauty or love. With the most charming of narcissists, this can be fun and entertaining to listen to – to some extent. However, in the workplace it soon becomes a regular feature and is rapidly tiresome and boring when you're a captive audience having to hear the same stories again and again... and again. Many narcissists I have met like this seem to have amnesia about what they've shared and you will hear the same self-indulgent recollections of the times they met famous or distinguished people (because they also love to name-drop). Or the time they won a big deal, or how much money they make, and so on and so on. Employees and colleagues, as a captive audience, are a great source of narcissistic supply. Narcissists need reliable sources of supply; this is attention, admiration, cheerleading, enthusiasm, awe, etc, in order to support their ego and feed the grandiose fantasies they have about themselves and their lives. A narcissistic manager or colleague will require this and will punish anyone who doesn't get on board with enough enthusiasm; maybe by being ignored, ostracised, gossiped about, belittled, humiliated, criticised, excluded, or through other ways of sabotaging them professionally.

Narcissists create a very toxic work environment. Places that support and ensure a healthy work environment leave little room for narcissists to play in and so, where there is not enough of an opportunity for supply to be met, these kinds of people actually tend to move on to companies, environments and people where they will get this from. You can go some way towards helping to safeguard your workplace from toxicity by focusing on fostering a healthy environment that is no place for people who want to disrupt it or cause trouble.

Being Special and Unique

You will spot narcissists in the workplace by how special and unique they believe they are. Because they are so special and different, they will also believe they can only liaise, work with, connect with other elite, special people or institutes.

Much like their sense of grandiosity, they will claim to have 'the most successful sales record ever', that they've been told they are 'the best project manager in the history of the company' and been trained or mentored by the best. Grandiose narcissists will shamelessly name-drop.

They arrogantly snub others because they are 'too busy and too important'.

They believe the business wouldn't run without them. In fact, as far as they are concerned the world would probably fall apart if it wasn't for them and their special and different skills and presence. They expect special and unique treatment and demand respect – even though they are rude and have little respect or regard for anyone else.

Strong Sense of Entitlement

As part of believing they are superior and special and different, narcissists have wildly unrealistic expectations. They have expectations around how they should be treated by people at work, both within and outside of any organisation. They expect others to comply with their expectations, wants, needs and demands. They also don't take too kindly to anybody who doesn't.

Jessica worked in a team in the office of a logistics company – alongside Anita, whose father knew the CEO. Despite being at an equal level in the business, Anita would arrive late for work most days and expect somebody else to make a coffee for her. She'd say she couldn't possibly be expected to work without her morning coffee. She'd try to delegate her duties to others in the team like they were her personal assistant, even though they were at an equal level. But she saw admin duties as 'below her'. When anybody took her to task about it she'd quickly remind them that her father knew the CEO and so she was practically part of the management team. Her behaviour was reported to HR yet, rather than show any self-reflection or humility, she was defensive and insisted she should have her own office. Her request was declined and she later left.

Envy

Those with narcissistic personalities tend to be very jealous and envious of others at work. They will not enjoy the successes or rewards of others. Instead, they will hate people for them.

Interestingly, they can be quite obsessed with the notion that others are jealous and envious of them. Regardless of if they are doing well or not, they believe that everyone else must be envious of them. This positions them as 'better' than others. Sometimes envy and sabotage can be masked as 'protection' or 'mentoring'.

Mistakes or wrongdoings at work can be blamed on this. They may claim sabotage by somebody who is 'jealous' of them. Some can be quite vitriolic in their attempts to ruin what you or others have or have worked hard for. They simply can't tolerate others having what they want and will go out of their way to sabotage this in one way or another or to take it from you. I have heard of cases in offices where toxic colleagues of this kind will deliberately go out of their way to delete files, or delete or rewrite the work of others, in order to sabotage and risk their projects or jobs. No regard given for the impact of that on anybody else or even the company. Just sabotage attempts through the green-eyed monster of jealousy and envy. It's a really ugly trait.

David was a rising star in his department, being a top performer and having earned himself an industry award. His boss Nick was keen to minimise and disregard David's achievements, though. He'd say things like, 'When I was in your position, I was too busy actually working to be bothered with awards and ceremonies – they don't even mean anything.' Nick started to cut David out of important and relevant meetings, saying that they were too serious or high-level for him. He didn't pass on an invitation to speak at an industry event and when David found out he was furious. Nick insisted though that he only had David's 'best interests' at heart and he was 'protecting' him by rejecting this opportunity on his behalf, insisting it wouldn't be a good idea and that it ultimately 'wasn't worth it'. Clearly, this was out of envy.

Arrogant

As we've covered, narcissists at work are highly arrogant in their demeanour and attitudes. The essence of the narcissistic personality is born out of a deep sense of shame and self-loathing. For narcissists, getting in touch with those feelings is so psychologically and emotionally unbearable that the narcissistic personality and all the behaviours that go with that serve to effectively keep this well at bay.

Arrogance is a fantastic way to steer well away from ever feeling shame or bad about oneself. It's literally a launch to the complete opposite end of the spectrum. Any narcissist will keep shame far away from themselves all the time they are being arrogant and haughty. This is why they are more or less permanently egotistical and rude.

Alex was always late for team meetings and never apologised. Instead, he'd announce that he'd been busy solving problems nobody else would be able to ever work out because his intellect was so superior! If there was an issue with any code, he'd mock the other developers and explain all that they were doing wrong. In one team meeting there was a review of a coding error, and it turned out that it was his 'superior and pioneering' work that had caused the issue. Instead of acknowledging his mistake or having the humility to address this, he blamed the whole system and complained that it just couldn't support his sophisticated and creative genius architecture.

Arrogance in the workplace highlights a superiority complex. Narcissists at work will dismiss other people's input or expertise and instead focus on their own self-promotion and means. People like this are highly rigid and defensive when it comes to acknowledging any mistakes or receiving any feedback.

Interpersonally Exploitative

Narcissistic bosses and colleagues will take advantage of others in any way they can to achieve their own gains. They are masterful at telling people what they think they want to hear. They will sweet-talk, charm, lie and cheat to make it to the top or to get what they want. Because they do not experience empathy in the same way as non-narcissistic people, they do not feel genuine remorse or regret. Without that, there really is little moral compass to guide a person through what is acceptable treatment of others and what is not. Narcissists see people as commodities and, rather than ever meet somebody and want to authentically get to know them or even attempt to have a mutual relationship, they think, 'What can this person give me?' If you bring a narcissistic boss or colleague potential contacts, connections, wealth, status, access to people or places, or you can give them adequate narcissistic supply, you're in. If you do not offer them something valuable or of use in some way, then you will be discarded and disrespected and treated as if you do not exist.

This is one of the reasons narcissists make fantastic sales-people. The more overt types exude uber-confidence and charm and will literally say whatever they think the other person wants or needs to hear in order to get what they want or to win a sale. They are highly persuasive. This often causes problems for other teams, who then have to deal with the fallout from not being able to fulfil all the promises and assurances the narcissist has lied to them about to secure the deal.

8

Narcissistic Abuse at Work

We have looked at the behaviours and characteristics of narcissism, as well as the narcissist in specifically a work setting. I hope this has enabled you to identify your narcissist boss, co-worker or client. Next, let's look at how narcissistic abuse can present at work.

Narcissistic abuse is the specific actions and impact of being in a relationship or situation with a manipulative, exploitative narcissistic person. Sometimes it can be difficult to recognise and name abuse while it's happening, so I will outline the typical harmful things narcissists do and give you some language to help describe what you might be experiencing.

Abuse is when somebody causes harm or distress, both directly and indirectly.

For example, **gaslighting** is where somebody says and does or denies things to the extent that it leaves you second-guessing yourself, doubting your own perception or reality. Denial, much like arrogance, is a powerful defence that narcissists use to keep their own shame at bay. To be on the receiving end of this can be confusing, cause you to question your own recollection or leave you feeling like you are exaggerating or being overly sensitive or unfair. If you ever accuse a narcissist of something you may see that their immediate, automatic defence is to deny, deny, deny. They are unable to take personal responsibility for their actions. It takes great humility for somebody to hold their hands up and admit and accept that they made a mistake or did something wrong or something that they are not particularly proud of – a narcissistic colleague will never do this.

Narcissistic abuse refers to the array of emotional and psychological manipulation tactics and abuse narcissists employ, as well as the impact their own psychological defences have on others.

With denial and gaslighting, your thoughts, feelings and experience are ignored, dismissed and denied. They are tactics a narcissist uses to protect themselves and being met with them is highly psychologically and emotionally abusive.

Another narcissistic defence is to **shame and blame** others. Again, much like arrogance and denial, pointing a finger at and shaming and blaming you or anybody else keeps any negative focus away from them. Shaming and blaming is cruel, unfair and abusive.

Narcissists at work will **lie and cheat**. They will lie about their qualifications, experience, abilities and achievements. They will report sales that are non-existent. They might steal or put in wild expenses claims. They will make up stories about other people to position themselves as superior and to put others down. It's very hard to believe much that they claim.

Rebecca, project manager

My narcissistic colleague would deliberately withhold crucial information until the last minute, causing projects to fail, then position himself as the hero who 'saved the day' by suddenly 'finding' what he'd hidden. He once deleted shared files before a major presentation, then 'discovered' the backup he'd hidden. I developed panic attacks, and struggled with work for two years after I left.

Narcissists also **tend not to respect people's boundaries** at work. However, this certainly does not mean you shouldn't have any. If anything, it's all the more reason to be firm about what you will do or not do. Narcissistic bosses and colleagues will have little, if any, respect for anybody's space, personal belongings or work-related boundaries. They will try to contact you with work issues while you are off sick or on holiday. Any disregard or disrespect of another person's boundary is a violation of their physical or psychological space and is manipulative and abusive, and healthy people simply respect other people's boundaries. That's how healthy relationships work. It's important to be firm with your own boundaries with work and, if you are off, to be unavailable. This is crucial to avoid burnout and we will cover more on this later.

Idealisation is a behaviour and manipulation technique where a narcissist will worship an individual or organisation – for as long as it serves them. Narcissists tend to view people and places in extremes, seeing them as good or bad, black or white. Idealisation means they will view a place or person as amazing, the best, someone who can do no wrong. They will rave about how great a person or organisation is.

Often alongside the idealisation phase comes **love-bombing**. Much like in romantic relationships, manipulative narcissists in a work environment will love-bomb in order to try to win the approval, attention and admiration of others. They may bring treats in for everyone, splash the cash with nice gifts, drinks and trips, or shower people with compliments. On occasion this may be due to a celebration and is, of course, a lovely gesture. However, when it seems too much or feels 'icky', it may be a way to try to manipulate others.

The cycle of abuse typically begins with idealisation and love-bombing, followed by **devaluation and discard**. The early stages are an attempt to assess who can be manipulated, who can be won over and what gains can be made from a person or institute. Depending on that, then comes devaluation, which is criticising, judging, belittling and shaming others. This can be subtle and gradual and done in a way that is not so easy to spot in the beginning. Like much abuse, it gets progressively worse.

At the stage of discard, a narcissist will have decided that you no longer serve them in the ways they want – either they realise they can't get what they want from you or you no longer provide them with whatever it was you once did. They will swiftly drop you. It can be cold and brutal. Narcissistic people genuinely struggle with appropriate endings and so they tend to discard and cut off people or places abruptly.

Narcissists in the workplace are notorious for trying to **divide and conquer** others in a group. The narcissist boss or manager really sets the scene for a toxic, stressful, unhealthy work environment by using these techniques. This is when they intentionally try to split people within the company or team. They may effectively plant seeds of doubt or suspicion in workers' minds about one another. They will create an atmosphere of competitiveness, mistrust and paranoia by favouring certain people over others at certain times – always to suit themselves.

This brings them a sense of being in control and having power over others.

The narcissist in charge likes to be the master puppeteer.

Abusive narcissists will try to **emotionally blackmail and exploit** others at work by trying to make someone feel responsible for their professional duties or mood. They aim to induce feelings of fear, obligation or guilt in order to manipulate others. They may use withholding or coercion, or be threatening or intimidating to employees. They will try to take advantage of, and use people at work, to serve their own ends.

Remember: what a narcissist tries to do and what they can get away with are very different things.

There are laws and legislation in the UK now that protect people against blackmail, harassment, coercive control and hate crimes within the workplace.

You can visualise a narcissist as a little fishing gnome; they will try to **throw bait** and hooks out for others to bite. Many manipulators are highly attuned to knowing exactly what bait to throw to catch each individual. These can include hooks like intrigue, guilt-tripping or fearmongering. It can be helpful to recognise and know for yourself what kinds of bait make you most susceptible or vulnerable. It might be your own feelings of guilt, or fear. Recognising and being aware of this is a useful first step. Learning how to manage whatever those feelings are to make yourself less vulnerable can be a game-changer. We will go through some techniques for how to do that in the chapter on boundaries.

Emma, HR assistant

When I raised concerns about workplace policies not being followed, my supervisor would say things like, 'You're just a junior, you don't know' or patronisingly say, 'You'll learn...' She'd also tell me I was 'being too sensitive' or, if I reminded her of what she'd said, 'That's not how I remember it'. She'd promise things in private then completely deny the conversation ever happened. I started recording our meetings because I began questioning my own memory and perception of events. Fortunately I wasn't the only one to see her behaviour.

Narcissists at work love to **project** their own actions or issues onto others. That is, they will accuse others of doing the very thing that they do themselves.

With narcissists, you will see patterns of behaviour around a **lack of accountability** at work. They also do not take appropriate or emotionally mature responsibility for themselves or their actions. Any issues at work, whether mistakes or interpersonal issues, are inevitably somebody else's fault, problem and responsibility, according to the narcissist. They will instead more likely position themselves as the victim and claim things like 'Everybody else in the team is being mean to me', 'I had nothing to do with that', or 'If she/he did their job then I wouldn't have had to do that'. Usually, they claim to have nothing to do with any errors or negativity but are the first to take credit for any positives or success.

Toxic people in the workplace sometimes try to use **slander**. They will attempt to create a sense of their own power and control by spreading rumours or lies about others. This is intimidating, frightening and controlling. This should be addressed directly.

Another typical narcissistic behaviour you will see at work is **topping**. The narcissist at work will not be able to stop themselves from 'topping' above and beyond what anybody else has achieved. You win a contract; they've already won the 'biggest contract in the history of the whole company'. It can almost be comical. Topping is a way for a narcissist to shift the focus, attention and admiration back to themselves, to feel bigger and better than everyone else.

Difficult people at work will also use **verbal abuse** to manipulate colleagues. This may be subtle and include **passive-aggressive communication**, communicating in an indirect manner or simply being problematic by not communicating much at all. Or it may be more explicit, like name-calling or criticising people either privately or in front of others. They can be undermining or demeaning. Often, doing this in front of others in meetings can be a very bold display of showing who is in charge. It is bullying. They may also try to control communication within the organisation, by not letting others speak or have a say or by trying to control who speaks to who. They may insist that they are positioned as the middle person and all communication must come through them. This is not an attempt to be helpful – they just want to control what people hear or know. It also positions them again in the role of master puppeteer. This kind of verbal abuse can be managed by insisting on a flat, open structure of communication within a company. This kind of structure also encourages a kind of ethos where difficult or abusive communication is called out and dealt with as and when it occurs.

David, finance manager

Our CEO would explode unpredictably over minor issues, then the next minute act like nothing happened. It was absolutely mind-boggling. Staff meetings were super tense and everyone walked on eggshells. I developed stress-related health issues and started dreading coming to work. The constant unpredictability was exhausting.

Narcissistic people are very **critical and judgemental**. They will, in a variety of subtle to bold ways, criticise, condescend and undermine others. You will also find that, while they are highly arrogant, they are at the same time highly defensive. So rather than be open to self-awareness, reflection or receiving and discussing feedback, they are instead very defensive in the face of it. Narcissists tend to be very sensitive to criticism or anything other than positive feedback.

There is no 'I' in team – but there are three in 'narcissistic'!

The narcissist at work is certainly no team player. They are typically all for themselves. They can be disruptive and create disharmony in a team – whether that is overt and explicit or done in more subtle, covert ways. At the very least, they will want to take credit for any achievements. They are arrogant and believe they are always right and, by default, you and the customer or client are wrong. They can be very rigid in negotiations. It's their way or the highway. Unfortunately, dealing with narcissists at work adds a layer of crap on top of trying to do your job.

9

The Impact

Of course, narcissism and toxicity in the workplace can have a profound impact on the organisation and for those working within it.

Looked at in the most positive way possible, aspects of healthy narcissism in business can confer some advantages in certain ways. The confidence, boldness, vision and drive of grandiose narcissists can give some businesses a competitive edge. Narcissistic leaders are charismatic, risk-taking mavericks. An aspect of this dynamism is sometimes the driving force behind successful novel start-ups and enterprises.

However, the darker side of narcissism and narcissistic behaviours, dynamics and abuse deeply contaminate a work environment. They destroy the culture, morale and confidence of those involved in it. When narcissism comes from the top, there is a toxic ripple effect that spreads throughout an organisation.

As we've seen, narcissism can present in overt, grandiose as well as covert, vulnerable ways – ranging from subtle undermining and attention-seeking to increasing levels of manipulation, control, aggressive dominance and bullying.

The narcissistic business partner is near on impossible to negotiate with. The level of stubbornness and arrogance more often outweighs any genuine business acumen. Arrogance and stupidity are a dangerous combination and one that unfortunately you may find in a narcissistic business partner.

Narcissistic leaders and managers initiate, from the top down, an unsafe, unsupportive, toxic work environment. The narcissistic boss – much like a narcissistic parent with their children and family – aims to create an atmosphere among colleagues of fear, mistrust and rivalry. They lie to and manipulate employees to get what they want out of them, making whatever promises they feel they need to keep them engaged in the process. There won't be any sense of stability or job security with a narcissistic boss. Instead, they prefer to stay in control by destabilising those around them with insecurity, worry, sudden or constant changes, or pitting employees against one another in order to divide and conquer the group. Needless to say, they don't care about their employees' well-being. All they are concerned with at work is what people can give them. They view members of staff as commodities and have no qualms about replacing people. The next person will be anyone who can be suitably impressed and in awe of them – thus providing them with narcissistic supply. As a result, there is often a high level of anxiety, stress, burnout and turnover of staff. Mistakes are punished and never forgotten about, while achievements are minimised. Selfish, self-absorbed people at work have an everyone-for-themselves attitude and don't care who they knock out of the way on their climb to reaching their goals.

The narcissistic colleague can really make your day-to-day

working environment deeply unpleasant. They may be obnoxious and entitled and are often lazy. They can be total energy vampires. They want to do the minimal amount of input on any team-related project, yet expect to take full credit. They are often negative, passive-aggressive, resentful, envious and jealous of any successes or praise anybody else receives. Some may even go out of their way to sabotage yours or the company's work.

Narcissistic customers and clients are pretty much a pain from the beginning. They expect special and unique treatment in any way possible. They are the customers who insist on negotiating an outrageous discount – and you find yourself agreeing and wondering why! They will expect to have access to you and contact you outside of office or working hours, and will push and not respect your professional boundaries. They are also likely to complain and become threatening if their unrealistic expectations are not met.

Narcissists at work always prioritise their own goals and success – while disregarding the needs or feelings of anyone else.

THE DISCARD CYCLE

The discard cycle is another typical feature and pattern of narcissistic abuse that you will find in the workplace. This is the same in both personal and professional relationship patterns. The abusive pattern starts with idealisation, followed by a devaluation stage before the final discard.

Idealisation The idealisation stage of the professional relationship is the workplace equivalent of 'love-bombing'. This can start right from the first moments of the initial interview. The narcissist will be trying to win the person over with compliments, praises and promises. This can feel quite intoxicating and make a person feel validated and excited. In the early stages of work, the narcissist will be trying to assess how much they might be able to take advantage by trying to manipulate them in this way. Naturally, we tend to respond well to somebody being positive and supportive; we feel connected, and idealisation can make us feel special and different. However, it can also mean we are in danger of being taken advantage of.

Devaluation The idealisation and love-bombing phase never lasts. Once the narcissist sees you are invested and engaged, their tone will start to change. This can happen suddenly, subtly or as a confusing mixture of the two. They start to gaslight you into questioning yourself. You start to doubt yourself and your judgement. At this stage self-confidence and trust start to crumble. Often, they have already set the scene for there to be some reliance on them. They become both the abuser and the soother.

Discard Narcissists at work want to be around people who help and support them to reach their own selfish goals and objectives, whatever they are. They devaluate a person and, as they become less useful to them, they will quickly and easily discard them. Narcissists do this to people who no longer serve them, or who they feel they can no longer manipulate. Discard is often cold and abrupt. It can come out of the blue and be a real shock to the system. As narcissists are unable to take proper responsibility for themselves, they will often try to frame the discard and end as your fault.

This cycle of abuse is shocking, awful and can be traumatising.

Needless to say, any workplace that is dominated by controlling, manipulative, divisive or abusive behaviours, where discard cycles occur continuously, is not going to be a healthy or fulfilling one.

A toxic work environment created by narcissists is unsupportive and is engaging in unethical practices. There is poor communication across the board, a lack of transparency, vision or sense of positive core values. There are lies, manipulation, bullying, harassment, discrimination and micromanagement, as well as staff favouritism and office politics. There are unfair and unrealistic work demands and pressure put on people and overall there is a lack of respect, recognition or reward. And often there will be a discard cycle that brings the situation to an end one way or another.

Jennifer, marketing

My manager would take credit for all my successful campaigns, then publicly blame and shame me for any minor issues. She'd change the project brief constantly, then act like it was me and I was being incompetent for not being able to read her ever-changing mind! I started doubting myself and my ability and developed anxiety and panic attacks before meetings. I went from being a confident, happy person to feeling like a fragile, nervous wreck before I left.

Being around destructive narcissists at work can rattle even the hardiest and most resilient among us. Narcissistic abuse in the workplace leaves people feeling undermined and undervalued. It negatively impacts on self-esteem, self-worth and confidence. It causes sleepless nights, stress, burnout and symptoms of trauma and PTSD.

Many people notice that when dealing with narcissists they feel as though their minds have been hijacked. Such is the power of narcissistic dominance in relationship dynamics; they demand all the attention at work and command your mental attention even when you're not at work. You might find yourself waking up in the night thinking about them. You might feel nervous, jumpy and on edge. Gaslighting leaves you questioning or doubting your own judgement, perception or even sanity. The division created among teams and colleagues can also leave you feeling paranoid, mistrusting, isolated and depressed.

Working with exploitative, manipulative narcissists in toxic work cultures can cause:

- Stress
- Anxiety/fear
- Depression
- Disengagement and lack of job satisfaction
- Low motivation
- Low self-esteem
- Low self-worth
- Chronic stress and burnout
- Exhaustion
- Symptoms of trauma, PTSD and complex PTSD
- Physical signs and symptoms of stress, e.g. muscle strains, aches and pains, digestive issues, problems with eating, difficulty sleeping, high blood pressure

Long-term exposure to narcissistic behaviours can lead to mental and emotional exhaustion and symptoms of post-traumatic stress disorder (PTSD). Experiencing this at work can be a replication of earlier childhood dynamics or a replay of narcissistic relationships occurring at home.

Workplace bullying and harassment tends to be a gradual process. In the early stages, it can be difficult to pin down as it may be subtle, veiled, indirect and discreet. Sometimes early warning signs are missed due to the excitement of a new role or the demands of the job. As time goes by though, more aggressive and blatant acts of intimidation, bullying and abuse occur. It leaves a person feeling confused, humiliated, ridiculed and isolated.

Stress and Burnout

Working with narcissists brings significant stress – there is no doubt or question about that.

Stress is both a physiological and psychological response. In small doses, short-lived stress can be helpful. A boost in cortisol and adrenaline can motivate us, sharpen focus, and help us get through important meetings or presentations. With short-term stress, there's a recovery period where we return to baseline, while chronic, ongoing stress, is neither helpful nor useful.

Signs and symptoms of stress include:

- Racing thoughts
- Difficulty concentrating
- Forgetfulness

- Rumination
- Mental fatigue
- Headaches
- Stomach upset
- Anxiety
- Irritability
- Feeling worried or tense
- Sleep or eating disturbances
- Increasing trouble switching off or relaxing

Chronic stress builds over time with less and less restoration or recovery. Long-term stress begins to negatively impact your productivity, mental health, well-being, relationships and physical health. If left unaddressed, chronic stress can lead to burnout – a prolonged state of physical, emotional and mental exhaustion. While stress is usually short-term and easier to recover from, burnout significantly impacts your ability to function daily and takes much longer to recover from.

Symptoms of chronic stress and burnout include:

- Inability to focus or concentrate
- Physical exhaustion
- Body aches and pains
- Headaches/muscle tension
- Chronic fatigue
- Sleep and eating disturbances
- Using alcohol or drugs to manage symptoms
- Irritability/mood swings
- Anxiety/panic

- Depression
- Inability to switch off or relax
- Losing interest in friends or hobbies
- No longer experiencing joy
- Hopelessness or helplessness
- Withdrawal from work and relationships
- Weakened immune system (frequent illness)

The World Health Organization's ICD-11 defines burnout as:

- Feelings of energy depletion or exhaustion
- Increased mental distance from one's job, or feelings of negativism or cynicism
- Reduced professional efficacy

Understanding stress and burnout helps you recognise where you may be on this continuum and take appropriate action.

Trauma and PTSD

Trauma describes the psychological and emotional response to distressing or disturbing events. Trauma is defined not by the event itself, but by the individual's experience. Often trauma develops when an event is too overwhelming for our brains to process in the moment, triggering survival mode rather than information processing.

Trauma is a normal response
to abnormal experiences.

Acute trauma tends to develop from single incidents such as:

- Road traffic accidents
- Violent crimes
- Natural disasters
- Medical emergencies
- Sudden loss or change (redundancy, break-up, illness)

Complex trauma develops from repeated, prolonged exposure to stressful, distressing, abusive or neglectful situations:

- Ongoing abuse (physical, psychological, sexual)
- Neglectful relationships
- Domestic violence
- Chronic illness

Vicarious trauma occurs when someone is exposed to trauma through their work or relationships (front-line workers, healthcare professionals, therapists, family members of trauma victims).

Moral injury causes psychological harm from witnessing or engaging in actions that violate your moral beliefs.

The Body's Response to Trauma

When faced with a threat to our safety or security, our nervous system activates primitive survival mechanisms. Our trauma responses include:

Fight: Confronting the threat with aggression or assertiveness. You become highly activated, tense, angry, possibly verbally or physically aggressive.

Flight: Escaping or avoiding the situation. This may mean physically leaving or mentally escaping through daydreaming, fantasy, or using alcohol, drugs or food to avoid feelings.

Freeze: An immobilised state where you feel overwhelmed, fearful, unable to think, speak or act.

Fawn: Trying to stay close to the source of threat (the abuser or narcissist) to survive. Essentially trying to please or align with them out of fear of abandonment.

Flop: Shutting down or submitting when you can't fight, flee or fawn. You feel exhausted and unmotivated and give up.

When our brains prioritise survival over processing, and the threat never truly passes (like with a narcissistic boss), trauma can remain unprocessed, leading to PTSD.

WHAT IS POST-TRAUMATIC STRESS DISORDER (PTSD)?

PTSD develops after experiencing or witnessing traumatic events. Anyone can develop PTSD from any stressful experience – not just war or extreme disasters. High stress, relationship break-ups, redundancy, bullying, harassment and abuse can all cause PTSD. It is a normal response to abnormal circumstances. Around 70 per cent of people will experience a potentially traumatic event during their lifetime. Up to 40 per cent recover within a year.

Symptoms of PTSD include:

- Re-experiencing the trauma through flashbacks (visual, mental, physical, emotional)
- Nightmares and night terrors
- Intrusive thoughts or images
- Severe emotional distress when reminded of trauma
- Physical symptoms (rapid heart rate, sweating, nausea)
- Avoidance of triggers, thoughts or conversations
- Persistent negative thoughts or beliefs about yourself
- Distorted thinking, self-blame, shame
- Feeling detached or disconnected
- Hyper-vigilance and hyper-arousal
- Feeling on edge or walking on eggshells
- Concentration and sleep problems
- Irritability or anger outbursts
- Self-destructive behaviours

Complex PTSD (C-PTSD)

Complex PTSD develops after someone has experienced repeated interpersonal trauma – betrayal, rejection, neglect, bullying, harassment or abuse over time. C-PTSD commonly develops from working for or being in a relationship with an abusive narcissist.

C-PTSD symptoms include:

- Difficulty managing emotions
- Depression and anxiety
- Issues with trust and safety
- Feeling like something bad will happen
- Helplessness or hopelessness
- Feeling flat, numb or empty
- Believing you're damaged, unfixable or unworthy
- Dissociation or disconnection from reality
- Thoughts of suicide
- Significant difficulties forming or maintaining relationships
- Chronic physical symptoms (inflammation, pain, fatigue, headaches)

How Do I Know If I Have Trauma or C-PTSD?

An assessment with a psychiatrist or psychologist can provide an official diagnosis. Self-report tools like the International Trauma Questionnaire (ITQ) are available online. If you're experiencing symptoms of PTSD or C-PTSD, it's important to seek appropriate professional support.

The Path to Healing

Understanding and recognising the signs and symptoms of stress, burnout, trauma and PTSD is the first step towards healing. These are all completely understandable impacts of dealing with narcissists at work. Learning more about how to deal with difficult, narcissistic people in the workplace makes a big, positive difference to your mental health and well-being. Mastering healthy boundaries, communication, self-care and self-compassion are key to this. Psychological therapy approaches like cognitive behavioural therapy (CBT), dialectical behaviour therapy (DBT), mindfulness and meditation, body-based approaches, exercise and lifestyle changes can all help with supporting recovery. We will look at some of the most helpful tips and techniques from these modalities throughout this book.

Please remember that stress, trauma and PTSD are all normal responses to abnormal events and situations. Healing is absolutely possible with understanding, support and helpful techniques and practices. It's useful to acknowledge and accept what is within your control and what isn't.

You can't change a narcissist, but you can change how you deal with them, how you interact with them and how much you let them affect you.

In time you can gently bring more focus to yourself and your own self-care and healing... and less to the narcissist. Before we go into ways to do that, let's look more deeply into narcissistic relational dynamics.

10

Relationship Dynamics

As we looked at earlier, narcissists have a pathological need for attention and admiration. They basically need a fan club. Anyone who leaves the fan club is at risk of being punished, ostracised, ignored, criticised in some way or subjected to a smear campaign.

Usually, the narcissist's requirements for adulation means they tend to move on to whoever or wherever can meet those needs. Ensuring your business is a healthy, open and supportive environment is one way to toxic-proof it from attention-needing disruptors – because if their needs are not met there they will move on. We will look into that more later.

Narcissists are especially attracted and attractive to a certain kind of person. This is typically somebody who can feed them with a reliable source of narcissistic supply.

As we know, narcissistic people do not take responsibility for themselves or their actions – and have no intention of ever doing so either. Therefore, it's a bonus for them if they can use somebody to **enable** them. This is usually a person who is very responsible – ideally overly – who is prepared to deal with the mess and trouble they create. It's essentially the same as the partner of an active alcoholic or addict, who, rather than challenge them, hold them to account or hold appropriate boundaries with them, instead quietly clears away the bottles or drug paraphernalia and makes excuses or justifies the other person's behaviour: *'They were just having a bad day...'*

Narcissistic people need to control and dominate relationships. They can do this unashamedly with brazen acts of selfishness, or, in the case of the more subtle, covert types, under the manipulative guise of vulnerability or 'care'. Either way, they seek people who that dynamic suits: usually the slightly more accommodating among us who are happiest with somebody taking the lead or taking up the space. This includes empaths, people with codependent traits or those who find they are repeating familiar relationship dynamics, e.g. they had or have a narcissistic parent or partner. As explained in my book *Raised by Narcissists*, it's not uncommon for adult children of narcissists to find themselves working for or with other narcissists.

There can be a 'comfort' in familiarity – however, what is familiar is not always necessarily healthy. We can often repeat a familiar relationship dynamic until we more consciously recognise that it is occurring and take steps to stop and change it.

So, the perfect 'fit' for a narcissistic boss, business partner or colleague is typically somebody who:

- is very empathic
- seeks to see the best in others to the extent that it clouds a realistic perspective
- has difficulty saying 'no'

- has difficulty asserting and holding boundaries
- has a distorted view or misunderstanding about what boundaries are or how they work
- is overly polite
- is fearful to speak up or 'rock the boat'
- is keen to 'keep the peace'
- is highly conscientious or overly responsible – to the point of taking on responsibility that is not theirs
- tends to minimise or neglect their own feelings
- is a compulsive caretaker, people-pleaser, fixer or rescuer
- is overly considerate of or habitually prioritises other people's wants or needs ahead of their own – to their own detriment
- has worries or fears about asserting boundaries or for asking for what they want or need
- has a strong sense of obligation that may get in the way of setting boundaries or attending to their own needs
- has difficulties with low self-esteem
- has issues with guilt or feeling bad – that get in the way of feeling comfortable asserting or holding healthy boundaries or holding others to appropriate account

A person with these sorts of traits is particularly attractive and useful to a narcissist, as they are easier to manipulate into taking responsibility for a narcissist's behaviours. They are more likely to enable these behaviours and to give them the focus and attention they want and need. A narcissist knows that, when a person is more focused on attending to them and not balancing that with their own healthy boundaries, they can be controlled.

Self-care and firm healthy boundaries are important and powerful protective factors when facing abuse.

Hope Versus Reality

Those who are ambitious to the point of being virtually blinkered by their dreams and aspirations are also at risk. Narcissists at work have a fantastic, innate ability to suss out and use somebody's motivation to manipulate them for their own gains. Narcissistic bosses and managers effectively 'love-bomb' employees with praises and promises of whatever may be important to you: promotion, training, promises of job or financial security, travel and so on.

With future-faking, there is a constant moving of goalposts and endless career-related promises that never actually materialise. Living in hope and fantasy rather than grounded reality is dangerous. It's so important to practise being grounded and taking a regular, objective realistic inventory and assessment of what your situation actually is at this moment – not what it was at the start, not what you've been promised it might be, nor what you hope it is or what you fantasise about. I've seen people spend years, if not decades, living in the hope of change or a narcissist fulfilling their 'promises' – only to find that it never comes.

Informed and Aware

There are certain characteristics that I believe put some people at a higher risk of getting pulled into an abusive and toxic relationship with a narcissist. Having grown up around narcissism can leave us vulnerable to repeating familiar relationship dynamics. It's not uncommon to find this playing out at work. Sometimes getting pulled into this simply comes from a lack of awareness or from inexperience. Very often people only become aware of narcissism and narcissistic abuse once they've experienced it and seek to understand what the heck that was about.

Dealing with a narcissist or experiencing narcissistic abuse is a wild thing to go through. It's hard to understand until you've been there. But once you have and once you do, you can learn a lot. It can help inform you for the future and propel you to arm yourself with awareness, information and the ways of being that protect you from ever going through this again. It can trigger a deeply healing journey of recovery and growth that ultimately can make it all seem worthwhile.

Being informed and aware of narcissism and abuse and the common vulnerabilities is a useful first step in awareness and growth. Then working on being able to say 'no', managing more effective boundaries and communication and letting go of any needs like people-pleasing, needing to be liked or habitually being overly responsible can really help to serve as protective factors to unhealthy relationship dynamics. See these skills as a **SHIELD** (we'll go through this acronym in Chapters 14 to 23) that helps protect you from the actions and impact of the toxic person.

11

The Toxic System

In toxic families, there is a typical kind of dysfunctional relational system with distinct roles and dynamics that repeatedly play out. The same can be found in workplaces. It can be helpful to familiarise yourself with this, as you may spot aspects of it at work and recognise colleagues or yourself in any one of the different roles. Becoming aware of dysfunctional systems and dynamics can help you to recognise them for what they are – and seeing them helps you to get some psychological distance rather than being completely absorbed within them. We can all get pulled into or adapt into one of these roles when we're in a toxic, dysfunctional group, but with information you can then step into conscious awareness and choice.

The Narcissist

This is the main, dominant narcissist in the workplace. There may be one or several main manipulators, to varying degrees, within the organisation. It could be the owners, investors, management or colleagues. Overt, grandiose or covert, more vulnerable types. In a large corporate company there's usually a mixture. The main perpetrators are typically selfish, self-serving and manipulative and treat others as commodities to be used to help them get what they want.

The lead narcissist is the person or people who largely drive the dysfunction and toxicity – they are controlling and manipulative and are master puppeteers of the others in the team or organisation.

The Enabler

The enabler is inadvertently a key player in the dysfunction and can be a sole person or the role of several people, to certain levels. The enabler in an organisation stands by and is a close ally to the main protagonist. Too afraid to recognise, admit or accept the dysfunction, the enabler is unwilling or unable to stand up to their narcissistic colleagues or hold them accountable for their own actions.

Enablers play a role in the dysfunction of an organisation or institution by allowing abuse to occur unchallenged. Enablers make excuses for sh*tty behaviour. They don't report it or stand up to it. They turn a blind eye, deny, minimise or justify the abusive actions of others.

'It's just our work hard/play hard culture.'

'Oh, it's just the way they are.'

'That's just their humour.'

'It's their age/culture.'

Some very high-profile and extreme cases of reported psychological and sexual abuse highlight the key role colluding enablers provide in protecting abusers. The cases of Harvey Weinstein, Jeffrey Epstein and R. Kelly, for example, include reports of significant sexual and psychological abuse and control that went on over many years. It was then documented that several staff members knew about the abuse, witnessed it or even helped facilitate it. The abuse happened in part due to the actions of enablers. Enablers are complicit in bullying and abuse.

There is no excuse for abuse and bullying and intimidation in the workplace. Or anywhere else for that matter.

Some enablers may have more awareness than others of their actions. They may also be victims of narcissistic abuse. For some enablers, their own trauma plays a role in why they may not recognise abuse for what it is, or why they may fear speaking up against it. Some enablers are incredibly fearful and compliant in the face of power and may have significant difficulty asserting boundaries or saying 'no'. Some people may find themselves in an enabling role without clear knowledge or intention.

For enablers, it's important to work on self-awareness and a grounded appraisal of their own part in any dysfunctional or toxic group dynamics. Awareness is key and, as you become aware of any enabling behaviours of your own, you can work on adapting to healthier detachment and more appropriate boundaries. This awareness can highlight any areas in yourself that may be helpful to work on.

Flying Monkeys

While we are on the subject of enablers, I will mention 'flying monkeys' and their role in a company. In the context of narcissistic abuse, the term refers to those who are also somewhat manipulated by and under the narcissist's spell. This may be a role you recognise or have even been unknowingly pulled into at work before. A flying monkey will spread the messages of the narcissist and continue their bullying and manipulation, often gossiping about, picking on and alienating individuals within an organisation. They might enable abuse by minimising or justifying the narcissist's actions. People can be flying monkeys because they are also narcissistic, but some may want to stay on the good side of the narcissist or be unable to stand up to them. Toxic work environments can create an 'each-to-their-own' survival mentality, and flying monkeys are a result of this. Some people will join in on the bullying in order to avoid being on the end of it themselves. It's a self-preservation tactic for many, but that doesn't make it OK. In fact, some people in this role may later find they suffer a moral injury and regret having not done more to stand up to the abuse. Being a flying monkey is another role in the dynamic that maintains abuse and dysfunction.

Chris, lawyer
My narcissistic boss would openly celebrate when competitors' employees were laid off, calling it 'natural selection' and 'survival of the fittest'. He'd encourage us to poach clients during their difficult times and would laugh about 'crushing dreams'.

He once fired someone on their wedding day 'for the story'. I developed moral injury and left the legal profession entirely. I still struggle with guilt over things I witnessed and didn't stop. And even sharing some of this now, I still wondered whether I imagined some of it.

The Golden One aka 'Employee of the Moment'

The narcissistic business owner or manager typically likes to have a golden, chosen person in the business. This is the person who can do no wrong (at least for a while) and is praised, put on a pedestal and highlighted to others within the organisation as the person to emulate. The narcissist will project themselves onto the golden one and may comment about how they remind them of themselves or how they share similar qualities. The narcissist will manipulate the employee of the moment by heaping praise and reward on them. There are often promises of promotion, or job or financial security.

Of course, it feels nice to have your efforts acknowledged and supported by a senior at work; however, a narcissistic, toxic dynamic means that this is done in a way that is problematic and manipulative. The narcissist wants their chosen person to 'behave accordingly' to maintain their position as favourite. The golden, chosen employee of the moment is also unknowingly used to create division and jealousy among colleagues, as others compete to be 'favourite'. The manipulative narcissistic boss can be quite strategic in how and who they choose for this role, and can and will change it at any time they want.

On the face of it, it might seem like a good thing to be the narcissist's favourite at work; however, this position is, unfortunately, rarely based on your own achievements – it's more about how much they can project onto and manipulate you. It comes with pressure. There is often envy among colleagues, separation and alienation and the golden one can often be left feeling like an imposter. It creates mistrust, rivalry and conflict among teams.

Some workers may aspire to be the golden one due to their own need for validation or in a bid to avoid direct confrontation. It is rarely as straightforward a position as that though, and it is a precarious position to be in. Narcissists will discard a person without any remorse or issue the moment they no longer serve them in the way they want.

The Lost One

In the typical toxic dysfunctional family system, the lost child is the child in the family who tries to navigate the chaos and avoid being in the direct line of narcissistic abuse the best way they can – by retreating and ducking out of the way. This is the child who hides out in their bedroom or gets lost in reading, fantasy or playing video games. The same role can be found in toxic work environments; the lost child is the one trying their hardest to comply and not stand out from the crowd. They will quietly conform, get their work done and try to avoid any conflicts or gossip.

In organisations they are often overlooked and undervalued. Others may take credit for the work they do. They tend to go unnoticed, and there are pros and cons that go with that. While on the one hand it is a means to avoid and evade the most toxic interactions at work, they may also go unnoticed to the point where they miss out on promotion or recognition, and they may feel unseen, unheard, ignored or undervalued. This may be a familiar role for the ones who adopt a lost-child position in the workplace, and may trigger old and unhealthy dynamics. Growing resentments can also build over time, and often the lost child ends up struggling with stress and burnout.

The Scapegoat

The narcissist uses scapegoating to deflect negative attention, blame or shame away from themselves and onto another person. Pointing a finger towards a 'scapegoat' in the office means picking on somebody to target. The scapegoat is usually the first or the most likely person in the workplace to recognise and name the dysfunction. It's an interesting dynamic but the narcissistic lead has a sense of who this person is. They are the least likely to be manipulated, and so the narcissist chooses the scapegoat to blame and project issues or failures onto them. They will try to plant seeds of doubt with others in the organisation, suggesting for example that the scapegoat is unreliable, untrustworthy or troubled in some way that means they are not to be trusted or believed. If and when the scapegoat does name any bullying, the scene and dynamics have already been set for others to dismiss them. The scapegoat is often the healthiest person in the sense that they are the first to see the abuse and dysfunction and to recognise it for what it is. However, as they are the only one identifying it, it can be an incredibly lonely and isolating position to be in. In the meantime, others in the toxic work environment are either narcissistic and abusive or, in an attempt to avoid abuse, aligned with those who are. Or they are the 'lost' workers, trying to hide away and avoid any conflict or drama.

Maria says:

I remember a moment in my old, highly stressful job, where I looked around at everybody in a meeting and suddenly had this realisation that I worked with my family incarnated. Even though we weren't related, I recognised the characters from my family, sitting around the room at work. There was the overbearing, larger-than-life, charismatic bully. This was my dad. And several subservient supporters, one or two sycophants – that was the rest of my family, too afraid to ever stand up or say anything to him. I remember looking at one colleague, during this meeting and seeing how she just seemed to stare into space – she was just disconnected from what was going on. It reminded me of my mother. She would often be staring into space, not present or aware of what was going on.

Others in the team competed for the approval of the narcissistic boss – wrestling to be the 'golden', favourite one.

I was the scapegoat. I was the one who called out the bullying and backstabbing and toxicity in the team – and I was ganged up on and targeted for it. It was like being attacked by a bunch of vultures who all turned on me. It was awful and really made me feel mentally unwell.

The best decision I made was to leave and be clear that I wanted to work in a healthier, more supportive environment.

The difference that has made to my stress levels and mental health is incredible. My advice to anyone in a toxic work environment is to get out and stay out. Especially if it's reminding you of your toxic family! I left home to get away from that; I don't want to replicate it at work now.

The most narcissistic person in the group is the main antagonist; others are then positioned or adopt different roles around them. They can be stable roles, or you may find that people take turns. For example, the narcissistic boss may aim to create rivalry and mistrust by choosing different 'favourites' to use for their own manipulative means. Arming yourself with information and recognising toxic systems can help you have more conscious awareness and choose how you respond to this.

12

The Drama Triangle

Another dysfunctional relational system you might recognise is known as the 'drama triangle'.

Developed by psychiatrist Stephen Karpman in the 1960s, there is a social interaction model called the 'Drama Triangle' that describes three dysfunctional roles people unconsciously adopt in conflict situations. It repeatedly plays out in toxic systems, whether that be relationships, with family or at work. The three key roles are:

The Persecutor: This is the critical, blaming and shaming, control figure who sees others as inferior or incompetent.

The Rescuer: This is the helpful, enabling figure who often has a need to be needed.

The Victim: This is the helpful, powerless figure who feels oppressed, attacked and seeks sympathy.

Let's think about how the drama triangle unfolds and appears at work. It's an unconscious process that plays out, but there can be an empowering shift when you learn to spot the drama triangle in action. Awareness is key to change. If you can recognise when there is an invitation to join the triangle, you can learn to no longer get pulled into this kind of dysfunctional system. There is an ongoing fluidity to the drama triangle at work. People will get pulled into different roles: some will willingly join in the dysfunctional system, some can rotate between the different positions, even within the same conversation! Each role feeds the others, creating a self-perpetuating toxicity that can poison the entire culture of a workplace.

Narcissists at work, whether they be the CEO or a lower-level worker, are adept at creating drama triangles because they serve them in several ways. Narcissists are controlling. The drama triangle allows them to shift their positioning, from a charming victim who elicits sympathy or support from others and meets their narcissistic supply needs, to an authoritative persecutor who demands compliance when it suits, giving them a sense of power over others in the workplace. While narcissists lack genuine empathy, they do often possess a keen ability to observe what triggers other people's emotions, so they will know which colleagues are natural rescuers, who are more likely to get pulled into a fixer-type role. Using this gives them the sense of control and power they want.

Let's examine the key roles within the drama triangle in more detail:

The workplace persecutor uses criticism and blame as primary communication tools. They will create unrealistic standards or deadlines or have constantly moving goalposts. The workplace persecutor is a bully. They enjoy intimidating and controlling others, they are micromanagers and humiliate workers in front of others. They are negative and harsh and view mistakes as deep character flaws that deserve punishment, rather than learning or growth opportunities.

The workplace rescuer constantly takes on responsibilities that are simply not theirs to take on. They have a view they are being helpful and will offer unsolicited help or advice. While this may appear altruistic, it often comes from a place of control. You can recognise controlling 'help' when they get resentful that their uninvited efforts are not appreciated in the way they want. Workplace rescuers are quite the enablers, and they will cover for others' poor performance or wrongdoings. The rescuer tends to get a sense of self-worth from feeling needed or indispensable. They can appear self-sacrificing and they have a need to be needed.

The workplace victim will use their 'helplessness' as leverage in conflicts. They will complain or share how they have been treated poorly by management or an individual or organisation, professionally or personally, to seek sympathy or support from colleagues. But they are not actually searching for effective solutions. Workplace victims rarely take responsibility for any problems or try to resolve issues; instead they seek to meet their attention-related needs by remaining victims.

The Rotation Cycle

You can see dysfunctional individuals at work shift between drama triangle roles. When a narcissist takes up the first position, there is then an open invitation to join the triangle by taking up one of the other roles.

Karen from accounts can go from spending the morning complaining about how unfairly she was treated by the finance director to aggressively criticising a junior's work in the afternoon. The victim position she adopts points to another as the persecutor and seeks to gather sympathy and support from the remaining position, the rescuer. The persecutor role then establishes power and dominance.

Jo, the marketing manager, may be a hero for solving an urgent crisis with a client but then complain to anyone who will listen about being unappreciated and overworked. The rescuer-hero showed their importance – they 'saved the day' – but they easily slip back into the victim role, again inviting others to offer validation or reassurance.

Max, a narcissistic manager, may harshly criticise somebody in their team in a persecutor role, only to then offer help and support. He quickly and confusingly switches between an abuser and a caretaker, a bully and a solution provider.

As a drama triangle begins, others will unconsciously be pulled into one of the other roles or even willingly join – some people love to rescue! Then people at work fall into triangulation, gossip, finger-pointing, taking sides, blame and all manner of toxic communication and dynamics. As the name suggests, the triangle creates drama and conflict – something narcissists thrive on whenever they interact with people. It involves manipulation and control and frankly it's emotionally exhausting. There's no place for drama triangles in healthy relationships or work environments.

The Drama Triangle in Action

It's important to understand the drama triangle because it's so synonymous with narcissists and dysfunctional relationships. It's a powerful dynamic people can find themselves pulled into. Your own power comes from being informed: familiarising yourself with the three distinct roles and learning how to recognise them in action. There will be an invitation to join and complete a drama triangle several times a day when you work in a toxic work environment, but empowerment comes from choice. When you are informed, you can simply choose not to join any drama triangle. It's a powerful way to protect yourself and avoid getting into toxic communication or conflict.

Recognise Your Pull

It can also be helpful to recognise which one of the three roles of the drama triangle are you most likely to be drawn into – we all tend to have at least one. Being aware of this can help you recognise and manage your actions. Do you feel compelled to help, even when not asked? If so, you may be more drawn into the rescuer position. Or perhaps you have a tendency to feel overwhelmed or unfairly treated? In other words, more of a default victim? Habitual persecutors tend to find fault with others' work and to criticise others. Honest self-reflection and awareness are key to growth and change. Being aware of your own tendencies as well as spotting them in others can help you to recognise the drama triangle and to then make a more informed, conscious choice as to whether you join in or not.

Practising the 'pause and reflect' technique is also a powerful way to manage pulls into a drama triangle. Before responding to any workplace drama or gossip:

- Take a breath and identify the roles others have adopted or the one you are being invited to play.
- Then ask yourself, 'What would a healthy, professional response look like here?'
- Choose your response consciously rather than reacting automatically.

The other thing that can help with managing the drama triangle at work is to develop boundary scripts. We are going to cover boundaries in more depth later, but for now it can be helpful to prepare some short, one-line responses for common drama triangle invitations.

For example, if you are invited into a rescuer role because somebody has positioned themselves as a victim you could say: 'I'm sorry you're struggling with that. Have you thought what you might do?' or 'I understand that is really difficult. What options or solutions have you considered?'

Or if there is an invitation for you to be persecutor, you might say something like 'Let's focus on possible solutions' or 'I'd like to focus on what we can do, rather than assigning blame'.

You can keep these prepared responses short and sweet. Then step away. Drama triangle invitation declined – and empowerment achieved.

The Empowerment Triangle

The empowerment triangle was developed by David Emerald as a positive response to Stephen Karpman's drama triangle. While the drama triangle maps out dysfunctional relationship patterns (persecutor, rescuer, victim), the empowerment triangle offers a healthier, more constructive framework for navigating conflicts and challenges.

The three roles in the empowerment triangle are **Challenger, Coach and Creator**, each representing a shift from reactive, drama-based responses to proactive, boundaried, empowered positions.

Challenger (instead of Persecutor): The challenger role transforms criticism and blame into constructive feedback and accountability. Rather than attacking or persecuting, the challenger holds people accountable, sets clear boundaries and encourages growth. Challengers ask tough questions and push for excellence, but they do so with respect and the genuine intention of helping others develop. They challenge behaviour and thinking without diminishing the person.

Coach (instead of Rescuer): The coach role moves from enabling dependency to fostering independence. Rather than swooping in to fix problems and rescue others (which only keeps them in a victim position), the coach supports, guides, and asks powerful questions that help people find their own solutions. Coaches believe in others' capability and empower them to take action rather than doing it for them. They offer support without creating dependency.

Creator (instead of Victim): The creator role shifts from help-lessness to empowerment. Rather than feeling powerless and focusing on problems, the creator takes responsibility for their choices and focuses on outcomes they want to create. Creators ask, 'What do I want?' and 'What can I do about this?' instead of 'Why is this happening to me?' This doesn't mean denying difficult circumstances – it means choosing how to respond to them with agency and intention.

Applying the Empowerment Triangle at Work

In workplace situations involving narcissists, the empowerment triangle provides a framework for maintaining your power and agency. Instead of being pulled into drama – feeling victimised, retaliating as a persecutor or exhausting yourself as a rescuer – you can consciously choose empowered responses.

When dealing with a narcissistic colleague or manager, step-ping into the creator role means focusing on what you can control: your boundaries, your responses, your documentation, your career decisions. As a challenger, you can hold firm boundaries and address inappropriate behaviour directly and professionally without being drawn into personal attacks. As a coach (to yourself or supportive colleagues), you can ask empowering questions: 'What do I need here?' 'What would a healthy boundary look like?' 'What's my next best step?'

The empowerment triangle doesn't eliminate difficult people or situations, but it shifts your relationship to them – from re-active and disempowered, to intentional and self-directed.

I used to rescue my colleague Alison constantly – she always had a personal drama or issue going on that she'd want to share about at work, and then because she was so consumed with her problems she'd constantly make mistakes – which I would fix! But when she blamed me for some errors that she had made and was trying to paint herself as the victim (yet again), I felt like I'd had enough.

I recognised the drama triangle. I stopped counselling and rescuing Alison and instead set clear boundaries about my own availability and responsibilities. I documented my work and, instead of covering up for her, I made it clear to our manager what was actually happening. Rather than feeling resentful and annoyed, I became the creator of my own experience, focusing on what I could control. The toxic dynamic lost its power over me pretty much immediately. I watched Alison move on to others in the office with her 'poor me' stories and just felt relieved to be free of it.

Action Plan

The next time you feel drawn into workplace drama, remember *you have a choice*. You can exit the drama triangle whenever you want, or not join in the first place. You can't control others' choices, or stop others engaging in drama triangles, but you can control your own responses. By refusing to step into any one of the dysfunctional roles and consistently modelling healthy communication and boundaries from the empowerment model, you become part of the solution. The workplace needn't be a stage for psychological drama. With awareness, boundaries and commitment to healthy ways of being, we can help create professional environments where people are empowered and thrive rather than merely survive.

13

From Recognition to Action

We've covered a lot in these first sections of the book: from understanding narcissism and NPD and specifically how this can show up in the workplace to recognising the typical traits, characteristics and behaviours of narcissists. We've also touched on the impact this can have when you're dealing with it at work.

Narcissism in the workplace is difficult, if not devastating, to experience. Individual ordeals will vary, yet having to deal with any selfish, manipulative, dishonest or tricky person is very challenging for anyone. In some ways though, it's become a bit of an occupational hazard in many professions.

A crucial first step in recovery is to acknowledge what is going on at work and the extent of the issue in a balanced but honest way. I'm sure some of you reading this are already there and are under no illusions about what you are facing. You may not need any further convincing. For some, our natural and psychological defences of denial may have buffered the reality somewhat. This is a perfectly normal, natural and understandable process.

Denial – as we've discussed – is a highly effective psychological defence that we all have. For narcissists, it is so off the scale that they live in a deluded fantasy land a lot of the time, unable to ever see the balanced, grounded reality of a situation or consider their part in it. For the rest of us... yes, we can still experience denial: it's a very natural, innate protective psychological defence, there to help cushion and soften the blow of a harsh reality for us. Denial works as a buffer, so we are not hit with too much in one go. This is what happens when we experience shock. There is the initial shock, disbelief, denial, then, slowly, over time, as we are more able to process intellectually, cognitively and emotionally, the denial defences ease as we become more able to take in the actual, factual reality of whatever it is that's happened or is happening.

At work, we may have an idealised version of an organisation or person. Perhaps we landed our 'dream' job (that later turned into a nightmare), and we don't want to believe it's not working out the way we had hoped. Or perhaps the business partner, boss or work environment are not what we thought they were. I've been there – it's devastating.

But it's important that we take time to pause and acknowledge our situation, so that we're not living in a fantasy that somehow it will all be magically OK, or that the bullying narcissistic boss will miraculously change. Sorry, but if they're a narcissist, they won't. Accepting the reality means that denial won't get in the way of you seeking change or moving towards something more fitting or supportive.

It can be helpful at this point to journal about what you have been experiencing. Put pen to paper and write about it. You could perhaps bullet-point specifics of what you've experienced or are currently going through. Or map out a timeline of events or behaviours. Write about how this has affected you. How might it still impact you now? What changes did it cause? How has it left you feeling about yourself and work? And anything else? Notice how that is for you. It can be challenging, or it may spark an urge to act and do something about it. Or perhaps you feel sadness or grief? Or anything else?

Know That It Is Not Personal

Understanding narcissism and the nature of narcissistic personalities helps you to know that it's a complex issue. The narcissist is not a happy, fulfilled or content individual, despite what they may claim.

You didn't cause it. The narcissist had issues long before you met them – and there's a high likelihood that they will continue to long after you've moved on. It's not your responsibility or job to cure it.

Narcissistic abuse *feels* personal. It leaves you wondering what you've done wrong. Absorbing a sense of responsibility is in some part a very common symptom of this unique kind of abuse. It's important to remember that it's not personal. Self-seeking narcissists will always be looking to see what they can get from others. It's just in their nature. Remember, master manipulators are highly skilled at telling people what they want to hear – especially in the early stages of meeting. Narcissists are chameleons, adapting to offer and provide what they believe each person wants or desires. This can only realistically be kept up for so long, though. In time their true colours are shown and become known.

If you have little choice now but to work with a narcissist, know that they are always going to be focused on their own goals. They will always ultimately prioritise their own progression and gains. Recognise that all their related behaviours are simply reflective of their issues. You can't control or change that.

What is within your control is what you do and how you take care of yourself. You can change what you do, and you can manage how you deal with them and how much you let them affect you.

PART THREE:

SHIELDING FROM NARCISSISTS AT WORK

14

SHIELD

Having to deal with a difficult narcissist in a professional capacity is something that I think is sadly inevitable for most of us at some point or another in our working lives. How toxic and troublesome narcissists are will vary, as will their position and the impact they have on us. In any case, there are some key practices you can adopt to help you shield from the narcissist and the effect they have on you.

In a therapeutic context, a shield is a set of psychological tools, techniques and practices that can help protect you mentally and emotionally from the effects of toxic people and their behaviours. Here, I have created an acronym model you can use to help protect yourself at work.

This professional shield includes managing your emotions; finding ways to self-regulate and stay calmer or detached when needed at work. It also includes taking good care of yourself and managing work/life balance, understanding, setting and holding healthy boundaries, which are always key to managing and ending toxic relationships. It's important this is clear and consistent, and we will cover more on how you can do this in a professional setting shortly. Ignoring the ego traps and bait is an empowering step in disarming the narcissist at work, as is learning how to empathise, remain appropriately kind and professional, yet, importantly, not enable any manipulation or abuse. We will also look at some practical pointers for logging interactions and delegating should things need to be escalated or if there is any potential for legal issues. There is also a reflective space to then think about deciding what is ultimately the best thing for you long term.

These elements of your self-protective practices can be summarised by the SHIELD acronym, and the following chapters will address each practice in turn. They are:

S – Separate emotions from interactions. Generally speaking, it gives you more power if you are able to find ways to manage your emotions around the narcissist at work. They thrive on triggering upset and emotional reactions. Staying calm and detached in your interactions with them helps you.

H – Hold healthy boundaries. Being clear and consistent in your boundaries is a key, game-changing way to manage and avoid difficult and toxic people at work.

I – Ignore the ego traps. Basically, don't bite the bait the narcissist throws out. A big part of being able to spot and ignore the ego traps comes from being informed about and aware of the behaviours and trappings of narcissistic behaviour.

E – Empathise but don't enable. You can acknowledge the toxic person's ideas, views or feelings without enabling, colluding or sacrificing yourself.

L – Log interactions. Keeping a note of any key interactions can be protective and may prove important.

D – Delegate and Decide. Know when it's time to direct issues to more senior people, or HR, or when to take legal steps or leave. Deciding what is right for you is protective and more power to you.

A fundamental factor to consider when addressing workplace toxicity is the effect stress and burnout can have on your health. Remember that:

Protecting your work/life balance isn't just important – it's essential, particularly when dealing with manipulative people and dynamics.

See Chapter 9 for an explanation of the key warning signs of increasing levels of stress. We will cover steps you can take and when to seek support in the next chapters.

Reflection Exercise

First things first: before we dive into how to shield yourself from a narcissist at work, let's explore your current situation. Consider how much time or energy you are giving to work.

How much do you think about work or co-workers outside of work hours?

When was the last time you took time off work without checking messages or feeling guilty?

Do you replay conversations, anticipate conflict or mentally rehearse defences for work?

Do you find you are regularly pushing through exhaustion?

How much of your self-worth is tied into your performance or productivity?

Does your workload feel sustainable for another year?

Is the amount of time and energy you are giving to work helping you to build the life you want – or taking from it?

Reflect on how much of this is absolutely necessary. Try to zoom out to take an objective perspective – and don't believe the narcissist at work's view on that!

What would your friends or loved ones or an understanding therapist say about it?

What would you think if this was somebody else?

What would you say if it were a person you really cared about?

Now, map out a pie chart of your life as it is currently and consider how much time and energy is spent on different aspects of it. For example: work, relationships, hobbies, health and wellness, travel, rest and relaxation.

Map out one more chart, this time for how you'd *like* it to be – a life that is healthy, or healthier, more balanced or more supportive of your overall well-being.

Notice what it is like to do this exercise. Are there any thoughts or feelings, beliefs or 'rules' that you notice around this?

Compare what this currently is to what you'd ideally like it to be, or what would be considered healthier or more balanced. Now ask yourself these questions:

What steps, however large or small, do you feel you can take now to address work/life balance?

What could you arrange or commit to do?

What would you like to do, that would be beneficial for you?

(It may be some enjoyable hobbies or interests that you've let drop or perhaps something new you'd like to try. Or somewhere to visit? Who would you like to spend more time with?)

Unhealthy/Unbalanced

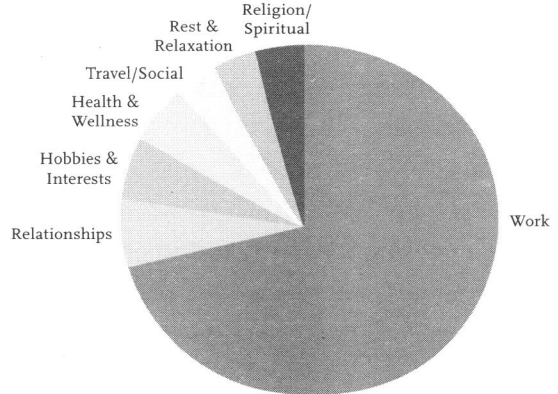

More Healthy/Balanced

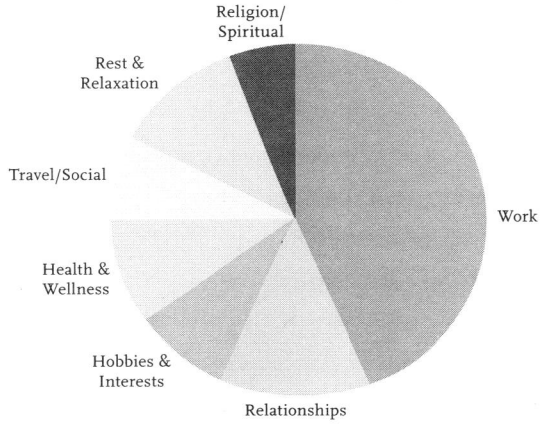

Commit to carving out time on a regular basis for more of these things and notice how this is for you.

You can also do the same exercise in relation to your sense of self-esteem and self-worth, in terms of where in your life you are currently getting these from. Most people derive a sense of worth and purpose from their work – there's nothing wrong with that. However ... if that's the *only* place or even the main place you are relying on getting worth and purpose from, then that is risky business when things start to change. It is much healthier to have several 'slices of the pie' and sources from where you gain a sense of self-esteem and self-worth, so they are not so heavily reliant on one thing.

Consider where else you might gain some sense of worth or esteem or purpose from. What roles do you have in life? E.g. as a son, mother, brother, partner, member of a community, a group, club, charity/volunteer worker, and so on.

Where is there valuable balance to be gained from?

Other helpful practices are to find any activity that absorbs your focus and attention for some time. This could be:

- an exercise or yoga class
- enjoying an engaging conversation or debate
- painting/drawing/colouring
- going to an art gallery or museum
- reading
- going to a comedy or music gig
- playing golf
- going on a group hike
- watching an engaging film or TV show

- volunteering to help others
- an arts or crafts class
- learning a new skill, for example learning to play a musical instrument
- spending time with friends and family
- visiting a new place or travelling

If there are any things like this that you used to do and no longer make time for that you'd like to pick back up, or things that you'd like to start... do it! The benefits will only be enjoyed by taking the steps and committing to doing something on a regular basis. Start today, even if it's just one thing, and notice how this leaves you feeling after a few weeks.

The most resilient people make time for play.

Reality Check

I want to share some harsh truths here about working for a narcissist.

They don't really care about you or your well-being. Please don't kid yourself that they do.

Narcissists experience and view people as commodities. Once a person has served their purpose as far as they're concerned, they will drop them like a hot potato and move on to the next.

Their actions are brutal – but remember, it's not personal.

They won't have any sleepless nights about your stress or

well-being. Ever. I'm sorry to say this but, if you drop dead at work, you will simply be replaced by the next person who can provide or serve them with what they want. It is not worth making yourself ill over.

Please don't fall into the trap of believing you are indispensable or that you're the only person who can do your job or bring everything you do to the organisation. Don't get me wrong – you have value, of course. But for your own well-being, try to keep a balanced perspective. One of the ways narcissists at work charm and emotionally manipulate people into giving them what they want is to convince them they are more valued than they actually are. They want people to feel special and needed, because that usually helps them to reach their end goals. Try not to let this manipulation pull you into doing so much more that it makes you overloaded.

As I mentioned before, narcissists bring an intensity and urgency to situations that pull people into crisis-management mode. It's highly stressful, yet at times it can also be exciting, dramatic and exhilarating. Some people understandably get a kick out of the highs of this. Working for or with a narcissist can be stimulating and a lot like being on a rollercoaster – there can be highs and lows; but, like a fairground ride, if you stay on for too long... it will make you sick.

15

S – Separate Emotions from Interactions

When workplace narcissists create their signature chaos, your nervous system bears the brunt of their manipulation. Separating emotions from interactions is the first step in shielding from narcissists. Recognising your stress levels and responses as well as understanding your window of tolerance can become crucial for maintaining your mental health at work.

Self-care and emotional regulation are essential tools for protecting yourself from toxic dynamics, and understanding the window of tolerance can help with this.

Your Window of Tolerance

The Window of Tolerance is a concept developed by Dan Siegel and widely used in some forms of psychotherapy as a useful model. You can think of your window of tolerance as a bandwidth. It is a space where when you are in it, you feel balanced, calm, composed and in control. It's a nice place to be! When you are stressed or triggered, your window of tolerance becomes very small. Ongoing stress may leave you drifting outside of your nice window of tolerance into one of two main states – hyper- and hypo-arousal. It may be gradual but, at times of sudden high stress or trauma, we are immediately propelled into a dysregulated state.

The challenge of emotional regulation intensifies when chronic workplace stress pushes or propels you outside of your window of tolerance. When you're hyper-aroused (anxious, panicked, irritable or angry) or hypo-aroused (numb, disconnected, tired, zoned out) you become more vulnerable to further narcissistic manipulation. This is precisely when self-care practices and emotional regulation techniques become your strongest defences. You can use mindful practices to notice and recognise where you are in relation to your bandwidth, and to help bring you back to within your window any time you find yourself out of it.

The Traffic Light System: Understanding Your Zones

You can use the traffic light system to recognise where you are at any time; there are green, amber and red zones.

The **green** zone is when you are well within the bandwidth of your window of tolerance. This is where you want to be – feeling balanced, present, calm and resilient. When you're operating within your window of tolerance, you experience a wonderful sense of being grounded and centred. Your emotions feel manageable, and you can self-regulate effectively. You can think clearly, respond thoughtfully, and maintain healthy relationships and balance. Here, you can work optimally. When you are within your window of tolerance you feel safe, connected, and capable of managing whatever life throws your way.

The **amber** zone is a warning, danger alert zone. This is a more activated, hyper-aroused state. When stress pushes you above your window, you enter a 'fight or flight' zone. The fight or flight response is when your nervous system kicks into activated, high gear, triggering rapid physiological changes: racing heart, sweating, racing thoughts, and a surge of adrenaline and cortisol – literally to prepare you to fight or flee. It is an innate survival instinct.

In the amber, hyper-aroused zone you experience anger and irritability, obsessive or compulsive thinking or behaviours, anxiety or panic or emotional overwhelm. When in the amber zone, you are also more likely to be activated into people-pleasing, fixing, controlling or impulsive behaviours, as well as feeling more drawn to self-medicating by using food or alcohol, or engaging in compulsive or addictive actions like shopping, gambling or sex.

This hyper-aroused, fight or flight response evolved to keep us alive during genuine, albeit short-lived, threats to our lives. In modern life, day-to-day stress and working in a toxic environment can leave us in a chronic stress state. Living in a long-term state of hyper-arousal can lead to feeling constantly 'on edge' and developing anxiety disorders, stress-related health issues, fatigue and exhaustion.

The **red** zone is a *hypo*-aroused state. This is when you drop below your window of tolerance, beyond a hyper-aroused zone and into a freeze or flop type response. This is another form of an innate survival mechanism. In the animal world, certain species freeze in order to stay alive; staying completely still often stops any predator's drive to go after them. Or they hibernate for their survival. The red zone is like this.

The red zone is basically your system's way of putting on the brakes and shutting down when you're overwhelmed. Here you may feel numb, disconnected, or completely exhausted. You can find yourself feeling flat, zoning out, feeling shut down or shut off. You think and feel like you can't do anything – 'I give up', 'I can't do it', 'I'm too tired'. In the red zone you feel like you want to retreat. You may feel chronic fear and mistrust. You may have a desire to just take to your bed and stay there for the foreseeable. It's like running on autopilot while feeling completely checked out from work or life. You can feel robotic and just 'going through the motions', shut down or ashamed.

Why Our Window Shrinks

We all have an individual window of tolerance. Some may have a wider bandwidth than others. Stress, trauma, poor self-care and a high level of life and work demands can all shrink your window of tolerance, sometimes quickly and drastically. Sometimes it effectively becomes as thin as dental floss – then it really doesn't take much to fall into either a hyper- or hypo-aroused state. Sometimes, as I mentioned before, we drift there as long periods of ongoing lower-level stress take their toll. At other times stress, triggers or trauma can suddenly propel us into an amber or red zone state.

Expanding Your Window of Tolerance: Building Resilience

Fortunately, there are practices and ways to expand your window of tolerance as well as practical tools to help you return to the green zone any time you find yourself, for whatever reason, outside of it. These include:

- **Breathwork**: Regular deep, slow breathing exercises calm your nervous system and offer protective stress reduction. I find one of the most effective techniques is 1-2 breath. This is where you exhale for twice the length of the inhalation. For a few moments now, try breathing in through the nose for a steady count of 4 and then exhale to the count of 8. It doesn't take long to feel the benefits of this powerful technique. Ideally aim to practise several times a day, every day, for five to ten minutes. You can do this any time and anywhere you want or need to.
- **Mindfulness**: Present-moment awareness creates emotional space, clarity and calm. Mindful awareness and observation is one of the most powerful and effective ways to help you return and stay within your window of tolerance. We will cover more on this in the next chapter.
- **Grounding techniques**: Grounding practises help you to

pause and anchor all parts of you in the here and now and are also very effective. One way to do this is to utilise the 5-4-3-2-1 technique. This is where you pause, take a breath, and take some time to use all of your senses to acknowledge fifteen things around you in that moment. These can be objects or colours. Mentally note 5 things you can *see*, 4 things you can *feel*, 3 things you can *hear*, 2 things you can *smell* and 1 thing you can *taste*.

- **Self-compassion:** Treating yourself with the same kindness and support you'd show a good friend or a loved one. Notice what you are thinking or how you are talking to yourself and consciously speak to yourself in the same way you would support somebody you really care about. What advice would you give? What would you suggest?
- **DBT skills:** Dialectical behaviour therapy is a psychological skills-training approach full of practical tools. One effective emotional regulation and self-soothing technique from DBT is to use self-soothing statements that you repeat to yourself and remind yourself; like 'I can cope', 'I'm doing my best', 'It's OK to rest', 'This too shall pass'.
- **Body awareness:** Take a moment to do a mental body scan. Notice how each part of your body feels. Focus on feeling where and how you feel your feet on the ground and work up through the whole body. Notice how your legs feel, your torso, back, arms and shoulders. Making slow movements and noticing how that feels can help you to reconnect mind and body and bring you into the present moment.

Working with Lucy, a narcissistic colleague, sent me into constant dysregulation. Her public criticism literally triggered hyper-arousal in me — my heart raced, my hands shook, and sometimes I'd snap defensively and then instantly regret it. Other times, I'd shut down completely, feeling numb and frozen during meetings.

My therapist introduced me to the window of tolerance. I learnt to recognise when I was leaving my optimal zone. When Lucy started her usual attacks, I'd notice my body's signals early. I developed grounding techniques: deep breathing, pressing my feet firmly into the floor, naming five things I could see, instead of listening to her.

Staying within my window meant I could respond rather than react. I set boundaries calmly instead of either exploding or collapsing. Lucy's behaviour didn't change much, she carried on being her usual vile self, but my nervous system's response changed. With practice I felt less reactive to her. I reclaimed my regulation, my power, and, ultimately, my peace at work.

Generally, ways to help you return to the window of tolerance from a hyper-aroused (amber) state involve doing more of what calms and grounds you.

Shifting from a hypo-aroused (red) zone usually takes doing more of what activates or stimulates you.

From a hypo-aroused red state, you can try:

- Movement. Get moving through walking, stretching, dance, do push-ups, jumping jacks or shake.
- Try a five-minute shake. Take time to literally just shake

out every part of your body. You can try this standing up or lying down or both. Shaking can be a wonderful way to shake off stress and release tension.

- Engage your body through mindful touch, tapping, massage or hugs. Self-massage with an invigorating oil can help, as can gentle tapping over your body with your hands or bamboo sticks.
- Stimulate your senses with uplifting or energising scents – for example coffee – or with textures, or music.
- Step outside for fresh air and invigorating breaths.
- Stroke a pet or animal.
- Try walking barefoot on grass to reconnect with your body.

Build Your Personal Toolkit

Experiment with different tools and techniques to discover what works best for you.

The key is practice – the more familiar you become with these tools, the more naturally you'll use them as and when needed.

Remember, spending more time within your window of tolerance isn't just more enjoyable – it's where healing, growth and genuine connection happen.

With awareness and practice, you can learn to recognise the early warning signs of drifting out of your Window of Tolerance or when you are propelled out of it.

Managing your emotional and physiological state in these ways is important anyway, but it's even more so when you're contending with the stress and trauma of narcissism or toxicity at work.

Practical emotional regulation tools can help you to regain balance, well-being and a sense of control at difficult times.

Whether personally or professionally, you can use these tools any time you want or need to, to gently guide yourself back to the green zone, where you will find better balance and well-being.

The Power of Mindfulness

Mindfulness is a tried and tested ancient practice and an incredibly effective psychological tool, which can help you to remain calm in difficult situations and develop some degree of healthy mental distance from intense emotional times.

Jon Kabat-Zinn – a well-respected teacher of modern mindfulness – defines it as:

'paying attention in a particular way: on purpose, in the present moment, and non-judgementally'.

It is essentially a practice of objective observation and noticing anything else that goes along with that.

It is an insight and awareness practice that can help you become the friendly, curious, objective observer of a focal point of your attention. Think of it as giving your mind a mini spa break. The practice of mindfulness is calming and restorative; and you don't need to sit cross-legged for hours at a time on a serene mountain top to experience the benefits. You can practise mindfulness any time, anywhere. You can be sitting down or walking. On your commute, on a break, or even for just a moment when you need to.

Just a few minutes of dedicated mindfulness a day is enough to feel the benefits. The focus of the practice can be anything: an object, an image or something at work. A good way to practise mindfulness is through observing your breathing (see page 171 for an explanation of 1-2 breathwork). Things get really interesting when you start to observe your thoughts or the actions of others.

The Benefits

There is a great deal of clinical research into the benefits of regular mindful meditation that highlights how it can help emotional regulation, as well as anxiety, stress, depression, symptoms of trauma, eating disorders and substance misuse. It's also been shown to be effective for managing chronic pain.

Remember you can dip into mindful awareness whenever and wherever you like. With more regular practice you will notice numerous positive differences, like reduced stress, increased focus and attention, feeling calmer, enjoying better-quality sleep and more. Studies also show that it can lower blood pressure and improve your immune function. It's a great self-care practice to incorporate into your daily life. I learnt mindfulness as a teenager and I can honestly say it changed my life – and it has helped me ever since. I practise daily and regard it as just another thing I do for a short period of time each day – just like taking a shower or brushing my teeth or walking the dog. Find the way that works best for you to incorporate into your daily routine.

I'd also like to add: it can help you deal with the narcissist at work.

How Mindfulness Can Help You at Work

Mindfulness can help with healthy psychological and emotional detachment from a toxic person and their behaviours. Practising mindfulness gifts you time, as well as psychological and emotional space. And this is important. It's a key difference in being able to *respond* rather than *react* to people, behaviours and situations.

Narcissists thrive on the stress and emotional reaction of others. Any display of this gives them more ammunition and a sense of power and control. You can be more effective in managing toxicity at work if you can manage your own emotional reactions so that you don't end up doing or saying anything that may be used against you. Narcissists are skilled at provoking people to bursting point, but the second you lose your temper, have an outburst, cry or show strong emotion, it is highlighted as 'proof' that you're the one with the issues and are emotionally volatile, 'too much' or unprofessional. This can leave you feeling more stressed and like you are damned if you do and damned if you don't. However, you can shift something powerful in the dynamic when you don't give them the reaction they are trying to get. You can achieve this by using mindfulness to help observe and regulate your emotions.

Let me be clear: this is not to say you won't have emotions – of course not. You're not a robot, and thank goodness you aren't. Psychologically and emotionally healthy individuals are aware of their feelings and give them the space and time they need. Being dysregulated from time to time and in response to situations or behaviours is perfectly normal too. The trick here is to manage this in the face of the narcissist at work, then take space and time to allow your feelings to come up – when it is safer to do so – with an understanding person or when you are in a safer place. Being able to regulate yourself and your emotions is a strength, to be used as a protective shield against narcissism or toxicity at work.

Next time the narcissist at work is provocative and says something that is irritating, ridiculous or triggering (as they do), instead of immediately reacting you can draw on mindful awareness to take a moment to get curious and just notice. Try this way of using mindfulness as a protective tool.

The STOP Technique

1. STOP what you are doing.
2. Take a breath.
3. Observe mindfully. You can mentally label what you've just witnessed or heard: the behaviour, action or even specific type of abuse or manipulation tactic (e.g. 'that's gaslighting', 'delusion', 'arrogance', 'false accusations', etc.). Then notice whatever else there is to notice in yourself or in others. Observe any thoughts that come

to mind, notice any feelings or urges or what happens for you physically. Use objective observation.

4. Proceed with conscious awareness, clarity, intention, choice and response.

Noticing creates space. You can observe whatever unfolds in the moment without being completely swept away in it all. This is a powerful tool for managing your emotions or reactions at work. With this comes conscious choice and you can then respond consciously and accordingly.

You can't control the narcissist. But you can control how you respond and deal with them.

Practical Tips

Start small: Committing a short while on a regular basis is better than nothing. Aim for a few minutes a day rather than a longer practice once a week or so.

Be consistent: Doing just five to ten minutes a day is beneficial. The more you practise the more benefits and awareness you may notice.

Find a place and time that works for you: Think of this as part of your daily routine, just like having a shower or brushing your teeth.

Try apps or guided meditations: If it helps you to get started or to try something different from time to time, you can try following apps for a guided mindfulness meditation. There's literally thousands to choose from on apps like Headspace or Insight Timer. I have also put together an online mindfulness course, which is available on my website www.drsarahdavies.com

Make it work for you: You can practise mindfulness while sitting having a morning coffee or when eating an evening meal.

Practice not perfection: The thing with mindfulness is that it's a *practice*. It's not about trying to achieve perfection. The aim is not for the mind to be completely quiet or not have any thoughts. The mind will have all sorts of thoughts; that's just how the mind works. The practice is the *noticing* of the thoughts, and the sense of space and distance that it brings you.

Mindfulness of Thoughts and Self-Talk

Mindfulness helps create a vast amount of awareness and insight, both internally and externally. Being more aware of your thoughts can help you recognise if your internal narrative is supportive to you, your emotions and your healing or whether it's harmful or adding fuel to the fire.

We all have internal chatter, an inner dialogue where we talk to ourselves in our minds. A lot of this is habitual and most of us probably don't really notice it until we consciously turn our attention towards it – which is exactly what mindfulness or awareness of thoughts can help with.

Narcissists at work and the ripple effect of toxic workplaces don't just cause harm to your daily work life or career. They can also negatively impact how you speak to and treat yourself.

Over time, the direct words and implications of narcissistic abuse, the criticisms and manipulation, wear down even the most resilient. Your internal voice, which perhaps started your current job with confidence and self-belief, may start telling you, 'I can't do this', 'I don't know what I'm doing' or 'I'm not good enough'. You may notice you start questioning or doubting yourself, or you're frustrated with, or hard on yourself. This kind of inner self-talk is not helpful. It's internalised toxicity. It happens when you are around negative, toxic people for too long. Negative, harsh or punitive self-talk is basically you picking up where others left off in terms of being mean to yourself. It does not help you with much. In fact, it is a sure way to make yourself feel worse.

This can be changed though, and mindful awareness is an effective way to do so. At some times our internal voice will be kinder than at others. The trick is to start noticing it more – and, if it's not helpful or supportive, change it to something that is.

Try to notice what you are telling yourself at work. If it's negative, it's often internalised messages from what we've been told in different ways by the narcissist. For example, things like:

'I'm a failure.'
'I'm not good enough.'
'I'm too sensitive.'
'I'm weak for letting this get to me.'

And so on. These are some typical types of thoughts we can internalise from toxic work environments. But please remember: thoughts are not facts. Challenge and change any unhelpful thoughts or self-talk by reframing them with something that is more supportive, compassionate and kind. For example:

> *'I was in an unhealthy environment at work – I'm trying my best – that's not failure.'*
>
> *'I am enough and I am doing enough.'*
>
> *'My sensitivity actually really helps me with my work – it's a strength.'*
>
> *'I am human and have understandable feelings. It takes strength to feel your feelings. It's completely understandable why I feel this way.'*
>
> *'I'm good at what I do.'*

Further Thoughts

Mindfulness is a relatively simple practice that offers numerous benefits. It's an effective tool to help with emotional regulation and a powerful resource to use for managing crap at work. It isn't about trying to become a Zen master – but it can help you develop a healthy relationship with your thoughts, feelings and experiences.

Our internal narrative is with us all the time and, whether we are conscious of it or not, narrating our experience and choices. If we have harsh, punitive self-talk then it's only going to make us feel worse and make it much harder to manage our emotions or to take good care of ourselves, including having and holding healthy boundaries at work or with difficult people.

Our self-talk can be changed though, so, even if you notice you are being hard on yourself, with mindful awareness you can take steps to replace any unhelpful self-talk with something more supportive, kinder and ultimately much more helpful. With regular work on this you will find that the more supportive, compassionate, good friend-type voice becomes louder. This is an important part of helping you manage difficulties and also recover from being treated badly.

Every time you choose compassion over criticism you reclaim a part of yourself.

The first step in shielding from narcissists at work is to **separate emotion from interactions**. Although it's perfectly normal and understandable to have strong emotions, try not to give the narcissist the feed they seek by showing strong emotional reactions. Most toxic people thrive on this and intentionally want to provoke it in others and then use it against you. Of course, it may happen from time to time. As I mentioned before, the aim is not to become an emotionless zombie – it's more about how you can better contain your reactions in the workplace to avoid giving the most toxic people ammunition to use against you. This also includes considering how you speak to and treat yourself. By using some of the tools I've outlined so far, you can help yourself to feel better, less stressed and more balanced.

The next step in shielding is holding healthy boundaries, so let's delve into this in more detail.

16

H – Hold Healthy Boundaries

This section is a big one, as it reflects the monumental importance of boundaries when it comes to dealing with narcissists at work.

Boundaries are your primary defence against manipulation, exploitation, stress and emotional exhaustion.

Your boundaries help protect you and your mental health from the narcissist's controlling or abusive behaviour. When I work with clients who are dealing with a narcissist in their life or are currently experiencing narcissistic abuse – whether from a partner, family member or somebody at work – we will always do a focused piece of therapy work around boundaries. Because mastering the art of healthy boundaries is one of the most effective ways to manage difficult, toxic people and relationships – anywhere. Understanding more about how boundaries work, specifically identifying your own and being clear about them, is a fundamental and powerful tool for managing narcissists and difficult people at work. Navigating workplace relationships can be challenging enough, but when you're dealing with a narcissistic boss or colleague and the ripple effect of that throughout the organisation, it's even more so. Understanding how to establish and maintain your professional boundaries is crucial for protecting and shielding your career, your work/life balance and your mental health. Put simply: holding healthy, firm boundaries will be the most transformative thing you can do to help protect yourself against narcissists, manipulators and, in general, idiots, both at work and in the rest of your life.

We all have three main types of interpersonal boundaries:

Psychological boundaries*:* These are your individual preferences regarding psychological matters: what you want to think about, talk about, give mental energy to or focus on. Psychological boundaries also include your choices and preferences in relation to what you want to share, what you think, your views and opinions, how you feel, what you believe and your ideas.

Emotional boundaries: Emotional boundaries work both ways: they reflect how you feel and what you share with others, as well as to what extent you allow other people to affect or manipulate you emotionally.

Physical boundaries: Physical boundaries are your individual preferences in terms of material and physical belongings and space: how much or how little and how you want to be touched, or not, or if you want to share your belongings or not, including your preferences around your workspace.

Regardless of where you are currently at with your

understanding and feelings about boundaries, there are steps you can take to improve or sharpen your sense of them – for your own benefit and for the quality of your relationships.

Healthy boundaries always improve and support your mental and emotional well-being and your relationships, both personally and professionally. Do not fear having them.

Most people respond favourably to healthy boundaries. They like them. They help people to know where they stand and to feel safe. This is one of the reasons most people want to do business with and be in relationships with those with clear boundaries. It feels good and it works.

Toxic people are the only kind of people who don't like boundaries. They don't like you having them and they don't respect other people's boundaries. They benefit from those who have none.

Narcissists and manipulative people are highly attuned to verbal and non-verbal cues that communicate our boundaries. Consciously or unconsciously, toxic manipulators sense who has firm, healthy boundaries and who doesn't. They are always inherently drawn more to people who have a poor or malleable sense of personal identity, preferences or boundaries. Narcissists have very little concept of healthy boundaries. They either don't have any, or they swing from having none to having extremely rigid, controlling 'rules' – always with their own selfish motives at the root.

Arming yourself with your own boundaries shields you from these people and the impact of their words and behaviours – healthy boundaries also act as a powerful repellent to toxic, narcissistic individuals.

They are also a strong magnet for more healthy people and environments. If you can get enough people on board in a business to establish, maintain and respect one another's healthy, appropriate boundaries then you create an environment where narcissists simply cannot easily exist. Later, we will look at how you can use this to protect your work culture. But for now, know that both professionally and personally:

Healthy relationships rely on healthy boundaries.

Boundary Issues at Work

Narcissistic behaviours and dynamics are similar yet present slightly differently at work than they do within a toxic family system or abusive personal relationships. However, the core patterns and strategies that help with managing them remain the same. Being able to set and maintain your boundaries are key throughout.

Let's name some of the ways in which boundaries are pushed or where these sorts of issues at work typically occur:

- Communication issues – the narcissist at work talks over people, ignores them, undermines, dismisses or criticises others. They purposely withhold or control communication and information. They don't respect communication boundaries.
- Toxic people create drama, unnecessary stress or conflict

at work. They will make it difficult to work collaboratively as a team.

- The narcissist at work has a need to be in control and so tries to micromanage others. They attempt to decide what you do and how much input you have, as well as control communication or information between people. They will try to manipulate individuals in a variety of ways to keep this control.

- Narcissists do not take any personal responsibility for their own mistakes, behaviours or decisions. Instead they blame others for any shortfalls, errors or failures.

- The narcissistic colleague takes credit for your or others' work or ideas.

- The narcissistic boss or manager will push their employees or team members' boundaries regarding work hours. They may constantly try to contact somebody when they are off sick or on leave, or outside of normal working hours.

- They push boundaries in terms of workload, by repeatedly putting too big a demand on people. They will use manipulation tactics like scaremongering, shaming or guilt-tripping so that staff take on much more than is reasonable. A culture like this can leave the baseline of what is a normal and reasonable workload looking deeply skewed.

- They play colleagues or business partners off against one another, showing favouritism and creating rivalry and mistrust. Here, they are attempting to position themselves as master puppeteer and ultimately be in control.

- They emotionally manipulate staff in order to serve their own selfish wants and goals. This typically includes some form of trying to induce fear and/or attempting to guilt-trip people.

Having your professional boundaries pushed in these ways understandably causes a great deal of stress and can ultimately push people to high levels of anxiety, depression and burnout. It creates such a toxic work environment and really hampers one's enjoyment of work and career progress. However, there are absolutely ways that you can manage your boundaries at work to be less impacted by this. Appropriate workplace boundaries highlight and weed out toxic, narcissistic behaviours.

The more effective we are at maintaining boundaries, the less room there is for toxic behaviours to thrive.

So let's take a look in more detail at what it means to hold and communicate your boundaries and how they can help you specifically in the workplace.

The Importance of Boundaries at Work

It is difficult, if not impossible, to try to set or hold boundaries at work if you are unsure of your own to begin with. So it's crucial that in the first instance you take some time to really think about where you stand on each of these areas and reflect on what is your preference and what is fair and reasonable. Our boundaries are like pizza toppings – they reflect our individual preferences. There are no rights or wrongs as such – it is just what you like, what you want or what you don't want. You decide for you.

Ideally, it's good to start off as you mean to go on and be clear about this from the beginning. However, you can also introduce or change your preferences and boundaries any time. Our values and preferences can change over time, and that's perfectly fine. You are the only person who is responsible for figuring out what your boundaries are for you. This is the first step. The next steps are communicating this to others and holding firm. Effective boundaries go hand in hand with consequences.

Having a strong sense of what your boundaries are aligns with having a clear sense of your own values and knowing what matters – or not – to you. With this comes confidence and protection for your mental and emotional health. With clear and firm boundaries, you are able to say 'no' much more comfortably. Being clear about your boundaries – both internally and externally – helps to keep people from manipulating or abusing you, as well as keeping you from doing the same to others. With a healthy understanding of boundaries in action, you can take good care for yourself and be clear about what is your responsibility and, just as importantly, what isn't.

Clear boundaries, particularly at work, means everybody is clear about what their roles and responsibilities are – and aren't. You know where you stand with firm and fair, clear boundaries and so it's a key fundamental relationship aspect that supports people in feeling safe and secure. Without clarity around roles, responsibilities or boundaries, it's impossible for either party to know where they stand or what is expected of one another. This creates a confused and confusing, muddled and chaotic dynamic. It also sets the scene for anxiety, stress, resentment, anger and burnout – all sure indicators that your boundaries are being pushed!

One of the key characteristics and behaviours of narcissistic people is a lack of understanding or respect around boundaries. They either have none, or they are extreme and rigid with their own – tantamount to having strict 'rules' with which they try to dominate and control other people.

As I mentioned before, narcissists do tend to sense and steer well clear of people who have a strong sense of personal boundaries. I have experienced this with my own growth. Having grown up around narcissism and all the inherited messages around boundaries and relationship dynamics that come with it, I was once a perfect candidate to be an ideal partner or employee to a narcissist. While it was deeply unhealthy, it was familiar and became a pattern that repeated until it got painful enough that I had to make some changes. Learning – or actually unlearning – the warped messages I had been taught about boundaries was my first step. I then sought to understand what healthy boundaries are and how they work, and then practised how to have them. It took change and a bit of practice, but I got there. As a result, my mental health significantly improved and my relationships in all areas of my life changed for the better. Not only am I no longer a magnetic attraction to narcissistic, manipulative people, I now seem to energetically repel them.

At one extreme end of the spectrum is having no boundaries, or very poor, flimsy ones; at the other is having incredibly rigid, inflexible, harsh rules. Neither extreme is healthy or balanced. A healthy middle balance is having firm, yet flexible boundaries. This is where you have a strong enough sense of what you like, don't like, want or don't want or what feels right and appropriate to you or not. And sometimes, when appropriate, there may be some small amount of room for flexibility, as per your preference, or if the situation or time warrants... or equally... not.

Your Invisible Shield

People with good, firm boundaries are simply not so easily manipulated. As I mentioned before, toxic manipulators tend to be drawn to people with flimsy or more easily manipulated boundaries. These might be people who are super polite and don't want to upset others by saying no or being firm. But please know: you can be nice and still have boundaries.

Narcissists have very little respect for anyone else's boundaries because they are basically too inherently focused on their own wants and needs. However, this does not mean you shouldn't have any – in fact, it's all the more reason to be sure you have them. Firming up your personal and professional boundaries immediately helps you to protect yourself further.

Our personal and professional boundaries form an invisible shield of protection around us. They communicate to others our individual preferences regarding psychological, emotional and physical matters.

They reflect our values, our self-worth and self-esteem. They determine who and what can get through. Our boundaries, for all of us, are essential for positive relationships and well-being. Boundaries help to keep you safe as well as providing clarity and containment to you and other people. Boundaries are beneficial to all parties.

The clearer you are in yourself about your boundaries, the easier it is to communicate them to others.

For all of us, our boundaries are intrinsically linked to our preferences, values and priorities. They reflect what is most – and least – important to you. Being clear about what *really* matters to you is a crucial fundamental step to then:

a) feel clearer about what is and isn't important to you
b) be able to communicate that more clearly to other people.

A valuable exercise is to take some time to consider what you care most – and least – about, in and out of your professional life. So let's consider this.

What's Important to You?

What truly matters to you – in your life, your relationships and your work?

What's super important here is that you assess your values – not what you think 'should' matter or what society says ought to matter, and certainly not what your narcissistic boss prioritises! Your values are unique to you and go hand in hand with your own personal sense of boundaries.

Below is a list of values to consider what is most and least important to you in your life, your work and your career. For each category, put in order of priority your top three for both most and least important. How important are each of these to you? And what does each mean to you at this point?

Core Professional Values:

Accountability – taking responsibility and ownership for actions and outcomes

Integrity – being honest and ethical

Excellence – striving to be the best and producing the highest-quality work

Respect – treating others and being treated with dignity and consideration

Authenticity – being genuine and true to yourself and your beliefs

Trust – being able to depend on others/being dependable for others

Honesty – being open and honest – both ways

Growth and Development:

Innovation – creating new ideas

Growth – focused on improvement – individual or shared

Resilience – being put to the test and bouncing back

Self-improvement – continuous focus on growth, your own and/ or supporting others

Mentorship/Management – supporting and guiding others' growth

Feedback – your level of openness to constructive criticism or alternative ideas

Challenges – how you feel about difficulties and challenges

Collaboration and Leadership:

Leadership – to take the lead and inspire or the preference to follow

Teamwork – want to work with others and be a valued contributor

Collaboration – how much you'd like to build partnerships and alliances with customers, for example and/or other organisations

Support – helping others to achieve professionally and vice versa

Empathy – understanding other perspectives and having yours considered and heard

Delegation – ability to delegate and trust others with tasks

Independence – preference for working alone or having sole responsibility for tasks

Achievement and Performance:

Results-driven - focused on measurable outcomes

Dedication – commitment to the goal and objective

Achievement – striving to accomplish meaningful goals

Persistence – not giving up when faced with obstacles

Competition and competitiveness – thriving with or aversion to

Recognition – being acknowledged for work and contributions

Goals – having clear objectives and working towards them

Personal:
Balance – maintaining healthy work/life balance
Autonomy – independence and self-direction
Flexibility – flexible work arrangements
Stability – secure income or environment
Passion – being excited and ignited about what you do
Sustainability – contributing to environmental responsibilities
Purpose – finding meaning in work contributions

Well-being:
Calmness – feeling steady and grounded
Contentment – feeling fulfilled
Fun – enjoying what you do
Peace - sense of calmness and tranquility
Pleasure – enjoyment and lightness
Health – physical and mental health
Status– your position or standing professionally

Add anything else that comes to mind and consider the values you've highlighted.

The clearer you are about what's important to you and what motivates you, the easier it is to consider and assess what is going to work or not for you. Age, life and circumstances may change this, so it's really worthwhile reviewing your values from time to time.

Reflecting on this may highlight that your current job, career or work environment are not fully aligned with your values.

For now, focus on what you value within your line of work and your role or position. Once you know what is important to you and what you want, it is easier to define boundaries that align with that. For example, if you value integrity and reliability, you will probably be keen to do what you say you will do and expect that from others too. Your personal boundary might be something around honouring that whenever and however you can. If your values reflect how important kindness and fairness is in the workplace, then your boundary might be not getting involved in unfair treatment or gossiping about or the bullying of others. Communicating that boundary might be simply stating 'I don't want to talk about this' or 'I don't know', or not getting involved in that kind of behaviour.

You can communicate your choices in verbal and non-verbal ways. You might make a clear statement or simply get up and leave, removing yourself from the situation. I used to do that whenever any gossiping started in groups at work. I simply didn't and don't want to be around to hear it or have any involvement in it. Me leaving every time communicated a clear message that I was not available for that behaviour. That's a boundary in action.

Remember – your boundaries are yours – and they help protect you and other people.

Your personal boundaries are about what is important to you and what matters to you – and additionally, what you will do should your boundaries be pushed or crossed by anyone else.

Good, clear boundaries go hand in hand with clear consequences.

If you value peace and respect you are unlikely to want to be involved in conflict or arguing. Your boundary, with an aligned consequence, might be something like 'I value respectful communication and peace so I will speak in a respectful manner. If you communicate disrespectfully and continue to raise your voice or shout, then I will terminate this meeting and leave.'

It's relatively straightforward. With clear boundaries you are communicating what is OK and what is not, as well as what your expectations are, and letting people know what will happen should your boundaries not be respected. How you communicate or word that is entirely up to you.

Importantly, healthy boundaries are not about trying to change anyone or control what other people do. Instead, they're about knowing your own boundaries, communicating them clearly, and doing what you say you will. It's crucial that you can action any consequences you state.

Areas of Work-Related Boundaries

Within a work setting there are boundaries relating to communication, workload and time, personal space, relationships, work hours, overtime, decisions and expectations.

Some areas in which you may want to consider your work-related boundaries could be:

- relationships with people at work
- work hours – breaks/lunch breaks/annual leave
- acceptable contact outside of work hours
- overtime
- your communication style and preferences

- appropriate response times
- how much you want to share about yourself with people at work
- how much you engage in gossip, personal or toxic talk with others
- definition around your job role or responsibilities
- being clear about what is not your responsibility
- delegation
- realistic deadlines and expectations
- your workspace and equipment/belongings
- physical boundaries/touch
- screen/digital communication
- personal social media connections with professional contacts
- passwords
- managing screen time and tech/digital overwhelm

Consider how you feel about each of these areas as well as any others that are relevant or come to mind. Identify what your ideal preferences and/or any deal-breakers are. Reflect on when you might have some flexibility and when it might be a clear 'no'. Take into account what is reasonable. Consider what your business partner, boss or organisation expects in these regards. If in doubt, ask. Don't assume what the other party expects or prefers. Being left to fill in the blanks or second-guessing can mean being at risk of getting it wrong. It's also a style of communication that narcissistic and manipulative people tend to enjoy and benefit from. They like to invite people into intrigue and guessing or mind-reading. A wonderful way to sidestep this is to ask direct questions with curiosity. Also, raising this as a clear and open conversation is a wonderful, healthy step in itself. It helps to manage expectations all round, and review and make clear where all parties stand. Clarity is healthy and takes away toxic intrigue or ambiguity. For each value, write a boundary statement and a corresponding consequence that you can and will action.

EXAMPLES OF WORK-RELATED VALUES, BOUNDARIES AND RELATED CONSEQUENCES

Value = Personal/family time. Work/life balance.

Boundary statement = 'So you know, I only check my emails during business hours or nine a.m. to six p.m. I'm not available to check emails in the evenings or weekends. If there is anything really urgent then either contact me via phone or reach out to [named colleague (delegate/signpost)].'

Consequence = 'If there is anything urgent I can be reached via phone, otherwise I'll respond to emails the next working day.'

It is important to action anything that you set as a boundary or action. Be consistent.

Value = Health. Balance. Boundaries around work hours and availability.

Boundary = 'I don't work through my lunch break. It's important to take breaks.'

Consequence = 'I won't be available for meetings or calls between one and two p.m.'

It's paramount that you do what you say you are going to do. If you say you are not available to take calls during this time, then do not answer the phone if one comes in. Better still, if possible turn the phone off and enjoy a proper break.

Value = Personal space and belongings. Material possessions.
Boundary = 'Please ask me before taking things (pens, papers, etc.) from my desk.'
Consequence = If this continues, you might remove items, keep them with you or lock them in a filing cabinet while you're away from your desk. Your boundaries. Your choice.

Value = Responsibility. Accountability. Reputation.
Boundary = 'It's not OK, and I will not be blamed for other people's mistakes or poor planning.'
Consequence = 'I'm going to document examples of this and escalate to management, HR or legal entities if necessary. I'll make clear what occurred.'

Value = Time. Communication.
Boundary = 'I'm going to need more time and information to reach an informed decision. I can let you know by the end of the week.'
Consequence = 'If you rush me to make a decision without proper information then it may be the wrong one. I will not take responsibility for a decision made in that way. So either you decide or you give me more information or time.'

You can document if insufficient time or information was given, as this is unreasonable.

The Fence Around Claire's Desk

Claire had always prided herself on being helpful. When her colleague Michael asked her to 'quickly check' his presentation at 4.30 p.m. on a Friday, she stayed late and did so. When he needed her to cover his client calls because he had 'an important meeting', she rearranged her schedule and helped out. When he took credit for her research in front of their boss, she told herself it must have been a misunderstanding.

It wasn't until Claire found herself working weekends to compensate for Michael's constant requests that she realised something was wrong. She reached out to me, reporting anxiety and stress. In our work together I introduced her to the concept of workplace boundaries – invisible fences that protect our time, energy and well-being.

'Think of it like a garden,' I said. 'Without a fence, anyone can trample through and take what they want. But with clear boundaries, you control who enters and what they can access.'

Claire started small. When Michael approached her with another 'urgent' task at 5 p.m., so he could head off, she took a breath and said, 'I can help you with that first thing Monday morning.' His friendliness and charm quickly shifted to irritation. 'I thought you were a team player, Claire.' He was trying to use guilt-tripping to manipulate her.

The old Claire would have caved. The new Claire recognised this for exactly what it is – manipulation.

'I am a team player during work hours,' she calmly replied.

Over the following weeks, Claire practised her boundary-setting like building a muscle. She stopped responding to

Michael's non-urgent emails after hours. She was strict with herself; even if she'd seen them, she wouldn't allow herself to reply until within work hours.

She documented their interactions. When he tried to interrupt her during focused work time, she politely but firmly said, 'I'm focused on something else right now. Can we schedule time to discuss this properly?'

She started limiting her interactions with him and would park his requests to discuss in set meetings.

Michael's behaviour escalated — he became more demanding, more stroppy, tried to go around her to their boss, and even attempted to isolate her from team activities. But Claire's fence held strong. She had learnt that boundaries weren't walls to keep people out; they were gates that she controlled.

Six months later, Claire was promoted. Michael remained in his position, his pattern of exploiting others finally visible to management. Claire's 'garden' — her work life — flourished because she had learnt to protect what mattered most: her time, energy and self-respect.

The fence around her desk wasn't visible, but it was now there and firm.

Key Points for Identifying Your Values and Implementing Boundaries:

- Take time to reflect on and consider your values. Personally, in relationships and in work.
- Review and reassess from time to time your values, what

is important to you and what truly matters – or doesn't – to *you*.

- From this, write down your specific preferences and boundaries in different areas of your work life.
- A helpful way to recognise if there is an issue, or a boundary is being pushed, is if you suddenly feel stressed, irritated or angry. If you notice this, try to articulate exactly what the boundary is.
- Be clear and specific with your boundaries – what it is you'd like, what you want, what works for you or doesn't.
- Be clear and specific about the consequences that you will action. Be clear about what you will or won't do in response.
- Communicate your boundaries and consequences calmly and matter-of-factly.
- It's crucial that you do what you say you will do. Follow through consistently.
- Boundaries without consequences are merely suggestions. Know that not actioning any named consequences only communicates that you simply don't mean what you say and won't do what you say you will. You teach people about your boundaries by your actions.
- Document any discussions about or issues around boundary agreements at work.
- Small steps. Gradually build your confidence by starting with smaller or easier boundaries and go from there.
- Embodying boundaries and feeling more comfortable with setting and maintaining them can take a bit of practice. In time it will get easier and hopefully, as you

experience the benefits of this, you will get to a place where you can state and hold your boundaries with increasing, and ultimately complete, ease.

Further Reflections

There can be misunderstanding about the purpose of boundaries. Some people may mistake having boundaries for a tool that's designed to control or change people or alter how they're behaving – it's not. You having boundaries at work may not stop or change the narcissist and their behaviours. However, it will help to highlight their actions and help you feel less impacted by them. Rather than trying to change them, you change what you do. Many people also fear having boundaries – especially at work. Sometimes people feel like it's rude or inappropriate to hold healthy personal or professional boundaries, or fear repercussions if they speak up. These notions often stem from early-life experiences, from time spent in toxic or dysfunctional systems, be it family or previous or current work environments.

Feeling unsure, anxious, or bad in any other way has the potential to stop you *feeling comfortable* setting and asserting healthy appropriate boundaries at work, so it's crucial that you find ways to manage those feelings. Clearing whatever has the potential to get in the way of you holding healthy boundaries is also a key part of the work. It's an area I spend a lot of time working on with clients.

17

Hold Healthy Boundaries:
Mastering Boundaries

Mastering the art of healthy boundaries, including feeling increasingly comfortable doing so, is genuinely one of the most beneficial, freeing, rewarding and protective things you can do for yourself, for the quality of your relationships both in and out of work, and for your mental health.

As you develop better boundaries, you can help yourself to feel safe and more contained and help those around you to feel the same too. You become less concerned or affected by what other people do or how they think or feel about you having boundaries. It's beneficial all round.

The only people who do not benefit from you learning healthy boundaries are manipulators, abusers and narcissists.

So, let's explore ways you can manage the usual suspects that get in the way of feeling comfortable holding healthy boundaries at work.

Clearing the Way for Effective Boundaries

How to deal with the FOG that gets in the way of holding boundaries.

Let's get curious about what gets in the way of you feeling comfortable setting and maintaining boundaries with other people, then get to clearing that out of the way so that it no longer interferes with your ability to do something that is essential for your peace and well-being. In this section we'll cover some of the usual suspects that tend to get in the way, and I will share with you some tools and techniques from cognitive behavioural therapy (CBT) to help you manage this.

I'm sure, at some point, we have all felt a wave of anxiety or dread when somebody at work has asked us to do something we don't really want to do. Or when we fear another person's reaction or the potential repercussions of us saying 'no'. It might leave us feeling as if we can't refuse. You may even recognise that horrible gnawing feeling of guilt that can creep in when we put ourselves first or leave work early (or even on time!) if we are not used to doing so. This is exactly what it's like to experience any one of the main trio of emotions that typically get in the way of feeling comfortable asserting yourself and holding firm boundaries. These are *fear, obligation* and *guilt* – otherwise known as the FOG.

And they're exactly like a fog – they cloud our vision and keep us stuck. Decisions that should be fairly straightforward, like simply saying 'no' or prioritising your own needs, are infinitely more difficult in the mist and cloud of FOG. That's why it's important to be able to clear it out of the way.

Narcissists in particular love to use the elicitation of fear, obligation and guilt to emotionally manipulate and control people. It's a classic trio tool for them. Learning how to manage these feelings within yourself, therefore, is another highly effective tool for being less impacted by a narcissist's attempts at manipulation or abuse.

Here are some practical ways to help clear the FOG and how you can use them to no longer allow these feelings to be used in a manipulative way against you.

1. Recognise the FOG

The first step is to try to spot and recognise the FOG as and when it's happening. Sometimes it can come on suddenly, perhaps in direct response to something the narcissist at work says or does. (Remember, they are master manipulators at doing exactly this!) Sometimes fear or a sense of obligation or guilt can creep up slowly. It may be subtle.

Take a moment now to think about when you last felt either fear, obligation or guilt at work, which then pushed you into saying nothing or saying 'yes' when really you wanted to say 'no'.

What happened?

What thoughts went through your mind?

How did it feel for you?

What did that feel like in your body?

Over the next week or so, try to make a note of any time you notice feeling fear, a sense of obligation or guilt at work. Ask yourself:
What happened?
What was the situation?
What was said or done?

Then write down what you felt – emotionally and physically. Make a note of any thoughts or beliefs you had at the time too.

2. *Understand the FOG*

If you notice, right about the time you feel anxious, obliged or bad, there will be a key thought that will have gone through your mind at the same time, or right before that feeling. The trick with this technique is to try to recognise the triggering thought. Our thoughts intrinsically and directly impact how we feel; so you can change how you feel by changing what you think.

Let's review some typical examples of how this can play out at work.

Fear

'If I don't say "yes" I'm going to lose my job.'
'What if they get upset or angry?' or 'They are going to be mad at me.'
'What if I fail?'

'What if they think badly of me?'

You will notice there is often a bad case of the *'what ifs'* when it comes to fearful or anxious thinking.

Our fears are usually about the fear of rejection, judgement, abandonment or conflict of some kind. You may believe on some level that setting and holding boundaries at work may result in you being disliked, disapproved of or punished. Some of these thoughts may be irrational or unrealistic.

Obligation

'I have to do this.'

'I can't say no.'

'I should...'

'I must...'

Obligation is often tied into an internalised sense of over-responsibility and moral duty. With this comes beliefs and thoughts along the lines of: 'I should...', 'I must...', 'Nobody else will, so that means I have to...', 'I'm needed, they need me...'.

These beliefs very often originate from the messages we've learnt or had modelled growing up, family roles or cultural or religious messages, or even from previous relationships or work environments. Obligation feels very much like a given, rather than a choice. Of course, we all have some obligation and respon-sibilities in a professional capacity, but too much and it can become an unhealthy bind and pattern of behaviour.

Guilt

'I can't say no.'

'I'm being selfish if I...'

'Does that mean I'm being lazy...'

'I'm a bad person if I don't...'

Guilt leaves us feeling like we are a bad person. Guilt can arise even when you haven't done anything wrong. A manipulative narcissist at work will say and do things to provoke somebody to feel bad – usually through guilt-tripping – which may be blatant or more subtle. When we are guilt-tripped, we feel guilty. Narcissists use guilt-tripping to emotionally manipulate you to do the thing they want.

In the context of work, narcissistic and toxic leaders aim to rule by fear and guilt. They will want to create a cloud of FOG across the office, for everyone in it. But you don't have to be clouded by it. You can clear the way for yourself. Sometimes fear, obligation and guilt are misplaced – narcissists use the threat of them to manipulate but, when tested, they may not hold up. It may be that our own experiences mean we carry a burden of fear, obligation or guilt. This typically stems from slightly distorted thinking adopted from past experiences, situations or relationships and not always from there necessarily being something to actually fear, or any wrongdoing on your part.

You can master some control over your thoughts to help yourself to feel differently, to feel better and to make holding boundaries feel more comfortable. This means you will stop allowing the narcissist at work to emotionally manipulate or control you.

3. Recognise and label the thought

Any time you feel any sense of work-related fear, obligation or guilt, try to catch the triggering thought before it catches you.

You can also label the category of the thought, as well as which kind of thinking habit it fits with.

We all have thinking habits and some are simply more helpful than others! Here are a few examples of the most common unhelpful thinking habits:

Catastrophising

'If I say no, everyone will hate me, I'll lose my job, then I'll lose my home...' – this is catastrophic-type thinking.

In other words, jumping to the absolute worst-case scenario.

You can recognise this as the fearful thought and mentally label it as 'catastrophising'.

How to counter this: Recognise that jumping to worst-case scenarios is not actually helpful or even realistic. Consider instead all other possible alternative outcomes, including the best-case scenario, and then consider what might be the most likely or realistic.

Mind-Reading

'They will think badly of me if I don't help.' 'They are going to think I don't know what I'm doing.'

This is mind-reading – believing we are somehow psychic and are capable of imagining or thinking we know what somebody else will think, feel or do.

How to counter this: Remind yourself that you are not actually a mystic psychic.

Instead, ask yourself if you are assuming or deciding already on others' behalf.

What's the evidence? What else could happen? What will it be like to wait to see what they say or do instead? Or even ask them?

Honestly, it's more than enough to manage your own thinking – there's no need to do other people's for them too!

A Case of the 'Shoulds' or 'Musts'

'I should do that piece of work...', 'I must do that...' etc. Thinking you should, or must, do or be puts inordinate pressure on yourself.

How to counter this: Ask yourself if you're being fair or kind to yourself or are you putting high expectations and pressure on yourself.

What might you say to somebody else in this situation?

Personalisation

'The boss is angry, he must be angry at me – it must be something I've done.' Assuming that it's personal is another unhelpful thinking habit.

How to counter this: Remember – it's not all about you all of the time. Consider what else might be happening for that person. Perhaps they are having a bad day or have other stuff going on that has nothing to do with you. A person's narcissism and abusive behaviour is also not personal.

Black and White/All or Nothing

'I'm either perfect at my job or a failure', 'The people at work all hate me', 'If somebody disagrees with me, that means they're against me'. Thinking in extremes – either all good or bad or in rights or wrongs – is an unhelpful habit.

How to counter this: Know that things are rarely all black or all white. There are myriad shades of grey in between. Consider where on the spectrum the truth could be. What is a more balanced perspective?

Critical Self

'I'm so stupid – how could I not see it?' 'I can't believe I made a mistake – I'm rubbish at what I do.' Critical Self describes the negative, harsh, punitive internal voice that judges you harshly, criticises you, blames and berates you. It can sound just like the voice of a narcissistic bully you've experienced.

How to counter this: Mentally label it for what it is. 'There's that internal bully.' Then try to counter this with a kind, supportive, compassionate voice.

Imagine what you would say to other people in the same situation or what a kind, supportive friend would say to you. What would you say to somebody you really cared about?

Remember: 'Thoughts are not facts.'

Challenge Unhelpful Thoughts

CBT teaches us that what we think affects how we feel, which in turn affects choices we make and the actions we take. You can learn how to recognise, challenge and change any unhelpful thinking to help yourself feel and do things differently around toxic people at work.

Any time you recognise you are feeling fear, obligation or guilt, or even some combination of all of these:

a) Recognise the most triggering, unhelpful thought or thoughts that go with that. Write them down.
b) Label what kind of thought it is, e.g. mind-reading, catastrophising, etc.
c) Question the thought. Is this thought based on objective fact? What actual, factual evidence do you have for this? What about for the case against it? If a friend of yours thought this in the same situation, what would you say to them? Try to think of alternative ways of thinking about it.
d) Replace the unhelpful thought with a different, more helpful and supportive thought – perhaps an even more realistic one.
e) Notice any changes in your feelings, any physical sensations or action you can take.

Experiment and Test

Once you can recognise any unhelpful or habitual thinking and challenge and change this, the next step is to start playing around with stating your boundaries and seeing how this goes. I'd really encourage you to test out and keep practising your boundary-setting. Start with small scenarios or interactions and, as a tester, try gentle boundaries.

One idea might be:

Fear: 'If I don't help out my difficult colleague, they'll get angry and punish me in some way.'

Test: Say 'I'd love to help with this, but I'm afraid I'm at full capacity for the foreseeable.'

Observe: What actually happened? How did that feel for you?

Further Thoughts

Narcissists are a nightmare to be involved with, but what often happens is much more underwhelming than what our fears might predict. I can't tell you how many times I've seen this with people I've worked with in my clinical practice. What they threaten is very different to what they can actually do. More often it's just our own fear that gets in the way of us feeling like we are able to hold healthy boundaries with them. What we fear most, rarely materialises. Fear, a sense of obligation, or guilt – FOG – really has the power to cloud your judgement and perspective and get in the way of you feeling comfortable holding appropriate professional boundaries. However, you can use the CBT tools outlined above to try to help manage these feelings by identifying, challenging and changing what and how you think. Then, in time, you will find boundaries becoming easier to implement. The more you can experiment and test out any potentially irrational or inaccurate thoughts or theories relating to boundaries, the more you will build up real-life evidence that will show that you can set boundaries without dire consequences or repercussions. Even if a narcissist balks or reacts badly to your boundaries at work, you can continue to set further boundaries and enact consequences, like in Claire's case. Practise this and feeling more comfortable focusing on yourself and your boundaries and self-care, and enjoy the emerging benefits and confidence that come with it.

Sometimes even the most toxic narcissists at work will sense a shift in your boundaries. Some may be provoked by that, but if you hold them consistently and firmly they will have little room to go anywhere. It only tends to highlight their toxicity even more. In my experience, more often than not in the face of emerging and healthy boundaries, a narcissist will find that they can no longer intimidate, bully, manipulate or get what they want from you. And instead of sticking around for a battle, they will move on to where else they can do so. This is because narcissists have a pathological need for power and control and to have their narcissistic supply met. The key is to work towards being consistent in your boundaries.

Cognitive behavioural therapy tools are powerful. You can use them to help you manage your fear, sense of obligation and guilt – or any other feelings that might get in the way of you doing what you need to do for yourself. Boundaries help protect everyone. Used with clarity and consistency they help everyone to know where they stand and feel safe. Narcissists at work will try to push them – it's just in their nature. But you don't need to allow this to sway you away from what you want or need to do. Keep focused on what is right for you.

As the FOG clears, you will notice more confidence and peace emerging within yourself. Keep practising these tools until they become healthy habits.

Next, let's explore ways to communicate boundaries at work.

18

Hold Healthy Boundaries: Communication

Communicating Your Boundaries

Just as your personal boundaries reflect your individual values and preferences, the way you communicate them is also your choice. For boundaries to be most effective, though, they are best communicated: *clearly*, *calmly* and *consistently*.

Be Clear, Calm and Consistent

Boundaries are most likely to be heard and received when they are clear, calm and consistent. Be sure to remain consistent with what you say and what you do. If you say 'no' but then allow someone to push you to change to saying 'yes', that communicates, quite powerfully, that you don't mean what you say. This is a mixed message you don't want to communicate.

Vague, ambiguous, hesitant or uncertain communication doesn't tend to work well either. Equally, there is no need to be aggressive or defensive. Try to keep it to the point.

For example, instead of saying, 'I'm not sure if I can work late tonight... I don't know if I can... maybe I could change my plans if you really need...' try to be clear, neutral and specific, with something like: 'I'm available today until six p.m., otherwise I can look at this tomorrow.'

Prepare for Narcissistic Communication Patterns

One of the ways a narcissistic boss or colleague will try to control the conversation at work is to suddenly start talking about something entirely different or random. An effective strategy is to prepare for this. Expect it. If you listen in meetings or conversations at work with a difficult, manipulative boss or co-worker, it probably won't take long for you to hear this sort of thing. Their aim is to derail, redirect and control the conversation. When you can recognise this for what it is, you can be more prepared and also take steps to not allow such a derailment to be effective. Good lines to respond with include: 'OK, that's great but right now, we're discussing x', 'That's a really valid point, but perhaps we can just finish or clarify this point?', 'Maybe we can come back to that, but for now let's stay with the subject of y...' or 'I just want to make sure I understand the point about...'

I've found it helpful to mentally visualise tracks and parallel lines around the narcissist at work. They won't want to stay within the parameters; however, you can nudge them back on track whenever they try to steer the conversation away from the task or topic at hand. Derailment attempts include suddenly talking about something else, going off topic, trying to start a drama triangle or even randomly making accusations. Accusing somebody of something (regardless of whether or not there's any grounds for it) is a typically effective way for a narcissist to try to put somebody on the back foot and take control of the conversation. This is because the very natural and instinctive response for most people, when accused of something they haven't done, is to immediately deny it and go on to correct them. However, the moment you get into this with a controlling narcissist, they have achieved what they are trying to do.

Again, an effective way to avoid this is to acknowledge what they've said, then remind them that actually, at the moment, you are discussing something else. Keep on track. 'By all means we can come back to that point, but right now... let us not get distracted from the topic at hand.' It takes some confidence to do this, but you can communicate it in whichever way feels comfortable. For example, sometimes I do this by being slightly self-deprecating: saying something like, 'I'm so sorry, my brain works a bit slower than yours... can we just be clear about this before we move on, I just want to be sure I get it.' The 'compliment' in there can sometimes be enough to temporarily disarm the narcissist – who, as we know, loves to be admired and commended.

Practice will help you feel more and more comfortable with managing these kinds of interactions and communication boundaries. It's ultimately so freeing and empowering.

You can also arm yourself with awareness and information as you get to know and recognise the favoured unhealthy, dysfunctional ways the narcissist at work is communicating. With this awareness, you can mentally label it as and when it occurs. This will help you to create a little more emotional space from the behaviour and to be more prepared for it whenever it happens. Recognise it for what it is – a dysfunctional person's dysfunctional communication.

Keep a Record

In my experience narcissistic people at work try to manipulate anything that has been said verbally. Narcissists will always have their own version of what has been said. Even if other people were present, narcissists will try to deny the conversation ever took place or to put words in your mouth, claim certain things were discussed or agreed and so on. It's generally good practice to follow up key communication in writing.

- Follow up verbal conversations or meetings with email summaries and keep a copy.
- Include phrases like 'as discussed in our meeting today'.
- Copy in relevant parties where and when appropriate.
- Keep the communication factual, to the point and professional.

It may also be helpful, prior to meetings, to prepare an agenda or talking points and make notes.

Top tip: This may become especially crucial at a later stage if any issues escalate into accusations or claims of harassment, or legal issues. Having a detailed record of examples of this kind of workplace harassment – and that is what it is – can be important.

Open, transparent communication will only irritate people who are trying to benefit from dysfunctional, controlled, 'pocketed' communication – but if you have a healthy sense of boundaries, how the narcissist at work feels about this is their business and in time will come to matter less to you. The important thing is that you are managing your side of the fence in healthy, open and transparent ways.

Consider Time Management

When considering your professional values and preferences around time management, it is important to regularly pause and reflect on what are realistic deadlines for any work or project. Not what the narcissist considers reasonable – as odds are they will be completely unrealistic and designed to set people up to fail to help themselves feel better! Consider instead what you regard as realistic deadlines for yourself or your team.

Communicate them and stick to them. If you are finding yourself having to consistently work overtime to accommodate poor planning, then that is an issue to recognise and address before it leads to serious negative impacts on your health and well-being. Remember you are responsible for this for yourself and it's important that you recognise your limits and set appropriate boundaries.

Narcissistic bosses and managers want to push people to their limits and beyond. They don't care about their staff's well-being. They are only concerned with supporting people enough to get to where they want to get to. Don't expect them to become concerned or step in to manage your time for you. As we know, they have very little concept of healthy boundaries, so instead will tend to just push and push and push. But you know your limits. Know that you are well within your rights to manage your own time, especially if it means protecting your well-being or the quality of work. That said, it's also incredibly important, in the spirit of mastering the art of healthy boundaries, to say 'no'; if you have enough on, then do not take on any more tasks – especially anything that is outside of your job description or remit.

Block out time in your work schedule to focus on what you need to do and hold boundaries around that not being interrupted unless there is an actual emergency.

As we've discussed, it is important to manage your boundaries around your office hours and communication outside of appropriate work time. Keep a note of what work you've done and when too, in case of any dispute.

Practise Professional Detachment

It's generally a wise decision to avoid getting into any kind of workplace gossip or drama – with either the main narcissist or any of their flying monkeys. It's toxic, it's unhealthy and it only causes conflict and problems. Narcissistic people, both overt and covert, as well as their enablers and flying monkeys, like to pull people into drama triangles and to listen to stories of how badly somebody has behaved, how awful another person is or how badly they've been treated. Getting drawn into this usually only backfires.

Be conscious of staying on your side of the garden fence. This means framing your boundaries in a way that emphasises your preferences and/or the consequences that are within your control that you can and will action, rather than communicating them in a way that points fingers or blames others. Accusations tend to be instinctively met with defensiveness. By using 'I' statements you can remain neutral, respectful and responsible.

Simple statements such as 'I'm sorry to hear that's happened, what do you think you'll do?' are nice ways to briefly acknowledge their experience without getting pulled into any kind of carer, fixer or counsellor-type role. This is avoiding getting into the drama triangle.

You are also communicating here that you are solution-focused and not available to indulge them about the problem or complaint. And questions like 'What are you going to do?' are quite subtle yet very effective ways of pointing out where the responsibility lies (i.e. not with you!). The next response they make to that will be either a suggestion of action or a declaration that they will do 'nothing'. Either way it will helpfully bring the conversation to an end.

Try to stay as emotionally neutral as possible in interactions. Narcissists feed off drama, upset and emotional reactions. If you consistently do not give them any of this, they do tend to head off and seek it elsewhere.

Stay Focused

Focus on the end goal and objective at work and with communications. Stay focused on the outcome or the objective of the communication, and less on the emotions. It can be useful to remind yourself that you're at work to get a job done or an end objective achieved. It can help to stay mentally focused on doing what you need to do professionally and untangling, detaching and protecting yourself from anything else.

Focus on facts at work, rather than getting pulled or pushed around by emotions or any of the typical dysfunctional communication that is designed to provoke upset, worry, fear or guilt or interpersonal issues. The grounding techniques and mindfulness practices I shared earlier can really help with this.

Another technique that can also help is to ask yourself what is most important. Will you be concerned about this or will this matter ten months or ten years from now? Try to keep your immediate and overall goals in mind – they're helpful and supportive for your own well-being.

Consider what you can and can't change and what is and isn't within your control. Stay focused on what you can control. You can't control a narcissist, but you can change how you deal with them and how you let them affect you.

Protect Your Energy

Limit your one-on-one interactions with the most troublesome people at work whenever and however possible. Ideally bring trusted others into any meetings or discussions. Restrict the open access troublesome people have to you. For example, I once had a tricky colleague who always wanted to pull me to one side to get in my ear with something toxic. Whenever she would approach me and ask for a minute to talk, I'd just reply in a light and friendly manner, 'Sure, we can talk here' – by which I meant in front of other colleagues. She soon stopped asking me because clearly she wasn't going to download her moans and groans in front of the others. And my boundaries meant she was no longer going to get access to me on a one-to-one private basis. Staying in a group can be protective.

Narcissists and their abusive actions can batter the confidence of even the most secure around them. The undermining, belittling and pushbacks can make it difficult to feel comfortable holding healthy and firm boundaries around them, and this is by design. You can strengthen your inner confidence and resilience around and in the face of this by consciously building on your internal narrative. This means reminding yourself:

I have the right to say 'no'.

My feelings and needs are valid and deserve respect.

It is for me to protect my energy, my time and my well-being.

I don't need to justify my boundaries to anyone.

I can trust myself.

Boundaries are not selfish – they are an act of self-respect and self-care.

I am strong enough to hold my boundaries – even when it's uncomfortable.

Other people's reactions to my boundaries are nothing to do with me – it's for them to take care of.

Setting boundaries gets easier with practice.

I am not responsible for managing other people's emotions – especially at work.

Take good care of yourself. Remember, self-care is not selfish – it's really important for our mental health and well-being.

Abusive, manipulative narcissists will always try every way they can to prevent you doing this. They will typically use attempts at fear, obligation or guilt elicitation to do so. They want to avoid and stop your healthy self-care because tired, stressed, burnt-out people are much easier to control and manipulate than people who focus on themselves in a positive and healthy way and protect themselves through self-care and appropriate boundaries.

You can practise self-care every day as well as whenever or wherever you need to. Self-care can absolutely be practised at work.

Take breaks whenever you need to help protect and recharge your energy, whether that's a proper holiday and time off, or a tea or lunch break. You may want to use some of the techniques for managing FOG we looked at earlier to help change any thoughts or beliefs that get in the way of taking time for yourself. There have been times when I've taken ten minutes to go and sit on the loo just to get a breather from workplace toxicity and regroup! Physical space can help with psychological and emotional space. So remember to come up for air, so to speak, if and when you need to.

Throughout the day, you can use stress-management breathing techniques, mindfulness meditation techniques or any of the window of tolerance tools. Practices like breathing or mindfulness exercises can be done any time at work without anybody even noticing.

THE GREY ROCK METHOD AT WORK

The grey rock method is a communication strategy that essentially involves appearing and remaining emotionally flat and unresponsive so that the abuser or manipulator will lose interest in you as a target or source of narcissistic supply. As I've mentioned before, narcissists have a need to feel like they have power and control over others, and seeing people fearful, anxious, upset or feeling bad about themselves gives them that. Emotional reactions feed the hunger of a toxic, narcissistic abuser. Using the grey rock method is a conscious self-protective tactic to emotionally detach – or at least not show the narcissist at work your emotional reactions, so that they lose interest, stop or move on.

To *grey rock* means to:

- Keep interactions short and sweet. Keep communication brief, to the point and professional.
- Stay focused on the objective facts or work-related information.
- Provide or share no or very minimal personal information. Do not give the narcissist any ammunition to use against you.
- Communicate with facts and information rather than opinions or personal views.
- Avoid showing them any strong emotional reactions. Demonstrate that you are unaffected by their toxic tactics.

That's not to say don't have any feelings; this is about using a self-protection tool for yourself, in the moment, to not show those feelings. You can note how you feel on the inside and maybe give yourself the space and time to process that later on, when you feel safe, perhaps when you are at home or away from work – maybe alone or maybe with a safe, trusted person. The aim is to not give the narcissist the emotional reactions or outbursts they are trying to provoke.

The DEAR MAN Tool

The DEAR MAN is a dialectical behaviour therapy (DBT) technique that lays out a guide for expressing your needs, saying 'no' and asserting your boundaries in relationships. The first step in the DEAR MAN skill is to identify your communication objective. Being clear about what you want to say or achieve in any interaction or communication can be especially useful when navigating and dealing with a narcissist at work who is masterful at diverting and directing the conversation. Beforehand, consider: What's my intention here? What's the aim? What do I want to achieve? What's the objective of this communication? Then use the following framework:

D – Describe the current situation, issue or concern or work-related task. Be clear, direct and factual. Keep it focused and professional. This can be short and sweet; just a line or two of a statement about the situation is enough.

Example: 'I know the deadline for completing this project is the end of this week... I understand the client is expecting it then.'

E – Express your thoughts and feelings Sharing these is an important part of boundary-setting, as it allows the person to understand how you are affected by what is going on. However, with a narcissist it is important not to get into a huge amount of detail or to give them anything they can use against you. Keep it professional and to the point.

Example: 'I recognise this needs to get done and I want to be sure it's done right and to the best of my abilities. I'm afraid I am feeling really under pressure and I'm worried about that affecting my judgement/ability.'

A – Assert what you need: State what you would like, want or need. Try to be as specific as possible, including with time-scales. Keep this direct and clear. It can be helpful to remember that other people are not mind-readers and toxic people in particular are too concerned about their own wants and needs to consider or attune to anybody else's. Try to be as clear as possible in yourself first, and then articulate and assert that clearly to them.

Example: 'I really need to get away on time this evening – so I'm sorry but I'm not going to be able to stay late today.'

R – Reinforce/Reward: As you articulate what it is you want or need, you can reinforce or reward the other person in a positive and respectful way, even if they haven't done anything to warrant it yet! This helps you communicate in a professional, respectful manner, even if others aren't. It also makes it difficult for others to come back at you with criticism or complaint.

Example: 'I know you have high standards and I really respect that; it's one of the reasons I am proud to work here. I also really appreciate that you want and support me to do my best work.'

M – Mindful Awareness: Stay present and focused. Being mindfully aware is being able to take a step back and observe objectively what is happening. This can help you notice manip-ulation tactics or anything else that might happen. Regardless, remain focused on your end goal. Don't get distracted. Don't allow the other person to derail or disrupt the ultimate objective. They may try – but with mindful awareness you can keep bringing the focus back to the topic. Ignore the distractions. Ignore the attacks. Ignore the manipulation techniques. Ignore the ego traps. If needed, just keep reiterating your point.

Note: Watch what happens next.

A – Appear Confident and Competent: Remember that our body language communicates a big part of the message we are trying to share. Prior to the meeting, take a few breaths and roll your shoulders to ease tension. In the meeting, stand or sit tall. Good posture can really help support you in feeling stronger and more confident. Use good eye contact and a confident tone of voice and be clear in your communication.

Remember: Speak confidently.

N – Negotiate: Be willing to negotiate in order to reach a solution to the problem or for yourself. This isn't the same as giving in and letting them have their way. It's an offer of some flexibility or a meet-in-the-middle that works for you. Consider beforehand what you might be comfortable with. Focus on what can realistically work.

Consider: If necessary and only if needed, be open and willing to some negotiation. Ask for forgiveness, not permission.

Reflections

It may feel like there's a lot to consider when thinking about boundaries at work and how to communicate them effectively. Wherever you are currently, keep reviewing your preferences and values, and practise asserting your boundaries at work. Start with less challenging colleagues to build your confidence. As you become more comfortable, try setting boundaries with the more difficult people.

If this is new territory for you or you're introducing boundaries to established relationships, expect some resistance – that's normal. The point of practising boundary communication in various ways is to discover how helpful and supportive they are for you, your relationships and your well-being.

It can feel scary and stressful to start with, especially with tricky or toxic people. Many people I work with report finding it tiring initially, but with practice and time, as you become more confident and effective at setting and maintaining boundaries, you'll find they're highly protective of your energy. You'll end up feeling freer and more energetic. With practice, it becomes easier and more comfortable, until it's second nature.

19

Hold Healthy Boundaries:
Resistance and Pushbacks

Dealing with Resistance and Pushbacks

As we already know, narcissists have some pretty strange ideas when it comes to boundaries. They do not embody healthy boundaries, by any stretch of the imagination. They only tend to have their warped version of a 'boundary' as and when it suits them. They really missed the memo on it being a respectful, useful, mutual exchange. Narcissistic people disregard, disrespect and push other people's boundaries, whether habitually, intentionally, subconsciously or unconsciously. Whichever way, one of the great things about you developing your own stronger sense of boundaries is that in time you will see that the narcissist's response matters less and less to you, and their manipulation attempts will impact you less too.

Please know that, regardless of how skilled you become at mastering the art of healthy boundaries, it's likely that a narcissist will still try to push them. But importantly, as you become more comfortable with maintaining your boundaries, whatever the narcissist does or doesn't do will matter less. Your invisible shield of protection means that what they do is their choice, on their side of the fence. It doesn't need to penetrate the fence and make you change or do anything differently, other than what is appropriate and fair for you to do. Narcissistic, toxic people, as we know, use reaction and manipulation techniques to try to get their way, but please know that that does not mean you need to withdraw your boundaries or your sense of what is right. If anything, it means you should stay steady and hold them even firmer.

Learning how to deal with pushbacks is a key part of this. Pushbacks can come in a variety of forms, including:

- passive-aggressive communication
- guilt-tripping – emotional manipulation
- overt questioning or challenging language or behaviour
- extreme emotional reactions like shouting, raised voice, name-calling, verbal abuse, hysterical or dramatic actions, accusations, threats etc.
- scaremongering – trying to induce fear or threat
- displays of anger and aggression

These blocks can range from subtle and discreet to extreme and outrageous – and everything in between. At least to start with. Until they learn from your words and actions being consistent that it's not going to work with you.

The following strategies will help you deal with a narcissist's pushbacks. Remember them and employ some or all of them whenever your boundaries are challenged.

Expect Resistance

In the same way as you can expect this from a toddler – which I'll explain more about shortly – you will inevitably get resistance from the narcissist at work, especially in environments where there may be some blurring of professional lines or in a culture where it's seen as normal. Some may be a little surprised or uncomfortable, or feel challenged by an introduction of boundaries. But that's completely fine. An embodied sense of boundaries means you can focus more on what *you* are doing and become less concerned about what other people are doing or how they are responding. If anybody has a problem with you setting and holding healthy, appropriate boundaries, that is their problem, not yours.

Healthy relationships and work environments rely on healthy professional boundaries

Key point: Don't take it personally. You can expect pushbacks and resistance. It reflects other people's issues, not any kind of failure on your part.

See the Toddler in Them

Narcissistic people are effectively emotionally stunted toddlers – try to see them as such. Visualising them in this way can be a really effective psychological tool that you can use to help you stand firm in your boundaries.

Like toddlers, narcissists are always instinctively – and at times incredibly creatively – trying to get what they want. Think of the example of a toddler who wants sweets and is told 'no' by their parents – they may employ a whole array of emotional manipulation tactics to try to get what they want. These could include:

- screaming and shouting
- temper tantrums
- whining
- being sweet and charming
- looking at you with puppy-dog eyes
- pleading and bargaining
- playing one person off against another (e.g. 'Dad never says 'no', 'Mum said I could have it')
- promises
- name-calling
- guilt-tripping
- silent treatment

and so on. Do these behaviours seem familiar?

Children trying to get their wants met is a perfectly normal, appropriate and necessary part of their age-appropriate development. The problem with adult narcissists is that, on some psychological and emotional level, they never really progressed past this stage.

As a parent, or any adult, would you let a toddler manipulate you in this way to get what they want, every time they want it? Would doing this be beneficial to them?

Children who are not taught or modelled proper boundaries end up learning that, if they scream, cry, bargain or throw their toys around and have a tantrum, they are given what they want. Good (enough) parenting means knowing when to hold firm and appropriate boundaries and knowing that to do so is absolutely in the best interests of the child. It's actually the most loving thing you can do. It's absolutely true for the narcissist, too.

Even though toddlers (and narcissists) will naturally use every one of the above tactics to push and manipulate you, holding a firm yet fair boundary communicates some very important messages. Namely that:

a) you mean what you say
b) you will do what you say you will – in other words you demonstrate integrity
c) you can take on board others' views and feelings, while still being fair
d) you have their best interests at heart
e) you care
f) you are safe
g) you are strong and not easily manipulated
h) your boundaries provide safety and containment.

In a similar way, you can stand firm in asserting and maintaining your boundaries at work by reminding yourself that they are appropriate and fair, and that by holding them firmly you are communicating some important information.

Remember: boundaries help people to know where they stand.

They are protective for both parties and help people to feel safe and contained.

The only people to have issues with boundaries are those who benefit from you having none.

Mentally Label the Type of Pushback

It can help to mentally label the kind of pushback you notice. This enables you to frame it in your own mind and get mental and emotional distance from it: 'Ah... there's that guilt-tripping thing they do.' 'There they go again trying to whip up a sense of urgency, panic and drama... this can actually wait.' 'That's them trying their charm offensive again... I won't fall for that this time.'

Seeing the tactics and techniques for what they are helps take the power out of them. Then you have the option to respond more consciously.

Have a Few One-Liners Prepared

Have a few short-and-sweet responses prepared for any pushbacks and give yourself time when needed.

I'm afraid I've already allocated my time for today with other things that need to be done:

'I'll get back to you about that by Friday.'

'I do understand this is urgent but I'm sorry, I can't do it right now.'

'I'm going to need a bit of time to consider and process that. Perhaps we can discuss again next week.'

'I think that's a great idea. Can you email me the information? Or can we schedule a meeting to discuss?'

'Let me talk to the others and see what they think.'

'I understand you're disappointed, but my answer remains the same (and I won't be guilt-tripped into changing my mind).'

'I am not available to discuss work matters outside of office hours.'

'I need a bit more notice.'

'If you want to discuss further then perhaps let's schedule a meeting with the others (HR, or other management etc.).'

Match Your Words with Actions

When your actions match your words, it communicates to others a powerful confidence and integrity. It says you stand firm and mean what you say and will action what you say you will. This is highly containing and appealing to healthy colleagues or clients.

Words are important, but actioning what you say you will or won't do is where the power is. It's imperative in the holding of firm boundaries that you action the consequences that are within your control in response to boundaries being resisted or disrespected.

If you say you won't check emails in the evenings or at weekends, then be sure not to! By all means do if you'd like to actually read them; but if you do, do not let anyone know you have, and be disciplined with yourself and only reply within set office or agreed work hours. You can schedule your replies to only go at certain times – be sure that is within the work hours you have stated.

If you say you need to leave on time, be sure to. If you say you won't engage in a conversation if somebody is raising their voice, be sure to state that, and if and when it ever happens, be sure not to engage and to leave the situation.

Key point: People will learn a lot about how to treat you by observing what you say and do. Sticking with your boundaries communicates a lot about what you will tolerate – or not. Generally speaking, people respond well to that. Sometimes even a narcissist will learn that there is little room for manipulation here and move on to another person they can get into that dance with.

Quiet Quit

'Quiet quitting' doesn't mean actually leaving your job. Instead, it's about doing the minimum that your job description and role requires – no more; you stick to your hours and main duties but stop going above and beyond. So you reject any extra demands, set firmer boundaries and focus on your main responsibilities. You do what you need to do – you get the job done and then leave.

This approach helps you to prioritise your work/life balance, protects your time and energy, and helps with managing and avoiding burnout – especially in workplaces where extra effort isn't valued or is taken for granted.

'Quiet quitting' can be a powerful self-preservation strategy when dealing with narcissists at work. Rather than overextending yourself or constantly striving for validation from those who thrive on control or manipulation, with quiet quitting you consciously choose to do your job well, while setting clear emotional boundaries and refusing to take on extra work or responsibilities.

By quietly stepping back from people-pleasing and focusing on your core responsibilities, you protect your energy, reduce exposure to toxic dynamics and reclaim a sense of autonomy in challenging environments. This approach supports your well-being without requiring direct confrontation, which can be especially valuable when dealing with narcissistic colleagues or managers.

Escalate When Appropriate

It's alarmingly easy when you are in a toxic work setting to lose sight of what is actually appropriate and what isn't! Especially if toxic behaviours, bullying or harassment, or a no-boundaries type of culture is an inherent part of the organisation. So it can be useful to remind yourself of what is and isn't acceptable to find a healthy perspective. Be prepared to speak up and escalate your concerns if and when necessary.

If you are finding that somebody at work is repeatedly pushing, disrespecting or ignoring your boundaries, despite you being clear with them, it may be that you need to escalate it and speak with somebody: a manager, director, somebody senior in another department, HR, an external supervisor or member of the board of investors, or any well-being services that are in place. It may even be that legal input is necessary.

When escalating, you can share your record-keeping of examples of inappropriate, unprofessional interactions.

In discussions at this stage, continue to communicate in as clear a way as possible, being clear about examples of inappropriate, unprofessional experiences without sounding too personal about it.

Remember: there are laws and legislation in place to deal with harassment and abuse at work.

KNOW YOUR RIGHTS

It can give you more power if you are informed as to your rights and where you stand ethically or legally in case things need to go further. Speak to any appropriate/available regulatory body, insurer, union or legal expert for advice. Do not hesitate to arm yourself with information and with knowing where you stand as soon as possible – even if you don't have to use this information, it will likely give you more confidence.

Breaking Point

Jacob had put up with his narcissistic boss Richard's belittling and undermining behaviour for long enough. He recognised it had taken a toll on his health and sought help to find ways to navigate and address it.

Jacob had rehearsed what he wanted to say to Richard. When the day came to do so, the words felt like stones in his throat. Jacob is naturally a peacemaker and never wants confrontation or difficulty, but he knew that at this point he had to make a stand. Not just for himself but also others in the team just as affected by the abuse.

For eighteen months, he'd repeatedly absorbed his boss's criticisms, undermining, humiliations, credit-stealing and gaslighting disguised as 'constructive feedback'.

As he entered Richard's office, his manager didn't even look up from his phone.

'What's up?' he said, without even giving Jacob the respect of looking at him.

Jacob's hands trembled slightly as he placed the printed email on Richard's desk – the one where Richard had blamed him, yet again, for his own missed deadline, in front of the entire team. The same email Jacob had just taken a screenshot of and forwarded to HR.

'I wanted to address this,' Jacob said, his voice steadier than he felt.

Richard finally looked up, with his usual smirk on his face. He sarcastically said: 'Address what, exactly? Your performance issues?'

A few months previously, Jacob would have immediately shrunk back, probably apologised, maybe even believed him. But something had shifted in the last week when he'd watched Richard attack and reduce Emily from accounts to tears over a 'mistake' that was his own miscalculation. He'd seen the abuse and the pattern clearly for the first time – the systematic blaming and erosion of confidence, the isolation tactics, the way he positioned himself as both the problem and the solution. He was vile and people had been too scared to stand up to him for too long.

'No,' Jacob replied. 'Your behaviour. The false accusations, the way you humiliate people, the way you take credit for our team's work while blaming us for your failures.'

Richard's face immediately changed. 'I think you're confused about the hierarchy here—'

'I'm not confused about anything.' The words came easier for Jacob now. 'I have documentation of every instance. HR has copies. I'm not asking for your permission to be treated with basic respect – I'm letting you know I won't take anything less than that any more.'

For the first time in eighteen months, Richard was speechless. Jacob felt stronger yet lighter than he had in years. 'I'll be following up our conversation with an email summary, copied to HR and discussing your bullying further with them. Hope you have a good day, Richard.'

As he walked towards the door, he heard Richard behind him scramble for words, but they no longer had the power to affect him. Jacob had found something that his boss couldn't take away – his own voice. He'd reached a limit and was holding him and his actions to account.

Jacob's experience captures that pivotal moment when you recognise the pattern of workplace narcissistic abuse and you can channel your feelings and energy into standing strong and firm in your morals, values and boundaries and stand up to the bully. Here you find the courage to stand up to and break free from the abuse. The key is often that shift in perspective – seeing the behaviour clearly for what it is rather than internalising the blame. When you grasp healthy appropriate boundaries, along with that comes clarity about what is acceptable and what isn't. You don't necessarily need to directly confront the narcissist. It may be that you take steps to report to others in more appropriate positions and let them do it. But you reach a point of your own limits and where you see the behaviours for what they are: abuse, and not at all OK.

Reflections

Dealing with resistance and pushbacks is simply a part of having boundaries. Healthy people respect, like and appreciate other people's boundaries. Dysfunctional, toxic, narcissistic and personality-disordered people don't. Instead, they tend to react badly to them and have an inherent desire to try to push or manipulate them. It is therefore realistic to expect some resistance and pushback. Focusing more on yourself and your boundaries allows you to become less and less fearful or impacted by how others react to them.

Remember the only person who has issues with you having healthy boundaries is the person who benefits from you having none.

Being met with resistance and pushbacks can be challenging, but it doesn't mean that manipulation tactics need to derail you from holding your boundaries. Remind yourself they are for the best. Boundaries are not about being inflexible or punishing – they're protective of your time and energy, and also reflect your values. Boundaries help your mental health and well-being, protecting you from stress overload and burnout. With practice and consistency, your boundaries will become an invisible shield around you, communicating to other people what is OK or not for you. This, in turn, helps people to know where they stand with you, and also helps them to feel safe in the relationship.

Keep practising. It will get easier to deal with pushbacks and resistance and you will feel better for it. They are energising and you will get to a point where you even enjoy it!

With practice or support, you can reach a point where you are able to stand up and speak up against abuse and park the responsibility for it exactly where it belongs, taking appropriate steps to hold the narcissist to account while taking care of yourself.

Ultimately your boundaries will help you to build a firm foundation for well-being, your professional relationships and your career.

20

I – Ignore the Ego Traps

The next step in building a shield from the narcissist at work is to recognise and ignore any traps of the ego. Usually we think of being egotistical as being completely and utterly conceited and absorbed in oneself. Of course, this is the narcissistic ego. The narcissist's ego is fragile and distorted and as a result fuels all the narcissistic behaviours and attitudes we're looking at here. One psychological theory is that everybody has an ego – it is a part of our personality and identity. Our ego is our sense of self and is the part of us that recognises 'I'. Having a healthy ego means having a grounded and balanced sense of self-awareness and self-worth. It allows you to have a sense of being separate from others and to have your own thoughts, ideas, beliefs and values. It also allows a person to set and maintain appropriate boundaries based on that.

Both grandiose and vulnerable kinds of narcissist are all about their own inflated sense of ego and self-importance. But as we all have an ego, in any kind of relationship there is an interplay between ours and the narcissist's. An important part of managing and moving on from relationships with narcissists or difficult, toxic people is to be aware of and then ignore the ego traps – both theirs and our own.

The toxic narcissistic ego is demonstrated in all the various selfish, self-seeking attitudes and behaviours we've seen in the earlier sections of this book.

Abusive narcissists will throw out all sorts of manipulation tactics and bait in the hope of catching their target or getting a reaction from them.

Learning how to recognise narcissistic bait for what it is, and – crucially – not biting, is a key part of managing and recovering from narcissistic abuse and is why I talk so much about it in the first part of this book. However, it's equally important to know when our own ego is provoked in this kind of relationship dynamic, because it may well want to join in. It's important to recognise this, as our own ego plays a key role in how we then manage these kinds of relationships or dynamics: specifically, how much we get involved and how much we are affected.

Our own ego gets involved when we believe we can be the person to change or control a narcissist or their behaviours. Or if we believe we can be *the* person to help or heal them – this is something inexperienced therapists can fall into with narcissistic clients. Here, it is our own ego telling us we are somehow responsible for the mood or actions of the narcissist. And it's for us to help or fix them.

Our ego is bruised if we get very offended by what the toxic person does or says, or if we believe it's personal. Our ego can get swept away if we go along with the charm and seduction of compliments, promises, declarations of us being 'special and different' or by the love-bombing attempts of the narcissist. It is also our ego that declares war if we are determined to 'put them right', or 'make them see', or if we aim to seek an apology or get into a battle to 'beat them'. Or if we enter into a power struggle with them.

All of these activated ego responses play a role in keeping us involved, be it trying to seek approval or ally with them, win them over, change or fix them, all of which leads to tolerating toxic behaviour for too long or engaging in an ongoing battle with them. Usually, it is much better to instead take steps to recognise narcissism and steer yourself away from it with compassion, wisdom and good, supportive self-care.

Much like narcissism, ego dysfunction is very much on a spectrum – from healthy ego to narcissistic.

A healthy, balanced ego allows you to have a grounded, realistic and balanced perspective of yourself and a situation or relationship. With a balanced ego you can recognise and accept your flaws or limitations – you have self-awareness and humility. Here we are open to feedback, change and growth. A narcissistic ego, on the other hand, is extremely defensive, self-centred and trapped by its own arrogance and sense of superiority. With a dysfunctional, narcissistic ego, there is very little room for personal insight or growth.

It can be helpful for your own self-awareness, growth and

healing to consider your own ego. In particular, it can open your eyes to any particular relationships or situations that activate a defensive, protective or reactive part of your ego. This may include people-pleasing or enabling. There is really nothing wrong with your ego kicking in and wanting to protect or defend you and your sense of self. This will happen, and it will certainly happen in response to narcissistic behaviour. Importantly though, it gives you even more power to be aware of what happens for you. You may wonder a bit about why, but I would say, more importantly, keep an eye on your own reactions, particularly any that play a role in provoking or maintaining a dysfunctional relationship with a narcissist at work. For example, as I have mentioned before, it's perfectly understandable to want to correct a toxic boss if they accuse you of doing something you haven't done. That can bruise our ego and a defensive part of us can want to put them straight. However, remember narcissists will believe what they want regardless. Narcissists will always stand by their own distorted version of reality. So instead of getting into a battle, please consider what may be more helpful to you in terms of taking the bait or ignoring ego traps.

To recognise your own ego-driven responses, take some time to reflect or journal on events or interactions that have happened at work. Write about what the antagonist did: what happened? What was the situation? What was said? Then, consider and reflect on what happened for you – what were your thoughts or feelings or urges? How did you feel in your body? How might this be ego-driven? What is your ego response trying to say or do? Did it feel like it was coming from the young part, or a healthy adult place?

Take some time to shine a light on this for your own insight and awareness. With mindful awareness of your own processes, you can put yourself in a more informed and empowered position to choose what you do next.

21

E – Empathise but Don't Enable

The workplace narcissist thrives on two things: admiration and accommodation. They are typically looking for others to give them narcissistic supply or to enable their abusive actions. It is not your job to do either. Whatever role or sector you work in, your responsibility is not and never will be to admire, enable or accommodate a narcissist or their abuse.

It's natural and understandable for some people to feel sorry for the colleague who constantly seeks validation, throws tantrums when challenged, or plays the victim when held accountable. Vulnerable, covert narcissists are masters at pulling on people's heartstrings or getting people to feel sympathetic to or responsible for them. The overt, grandiose types can also offer enough snippets of something that can leave you thinking, 'They must be insecure or hurting underneath' or 'Maybe they had a difficult childhood – it's not their fault.' And maybe you're right. But it's still not your problem to solve.

> Remember: you did not cause their
> dysfunction. You can't control it. And it
> isn't for you to try to change it or fix it.

The hard truth is that narcissists at work will exploit your kindness, manipulate your empathy into compliance or caretaking and turn your understanding into their ongoing get-out-of-jail-free card. They will avoid taking accountability for their actions. Narcissists will do this with charm, charisma or bullying and intimidation, as well as every manipulation tactic in between.

Please know that, as discussed earlier, every time you make excuses for their behaviour, or collude or cover up their actions, or enable them, you're not helping them grow – you're helping them avoid appropriate responsibility and any necessary consequences.

Knowing the difference between empathy and enabling is crucial in further protecting and shielding yourself from toxic behaviours at work. So let's be clear:

Empathy is the ability to understand and share the feelings of another. You can be empathic and still not take responsibility. You can have empathy and still hold people to account. You can have empathy without getting pulled into enabling, caretaking, fixing or people-pleasing behaviours.

Enabling is supporting another person to continue toxic or harmful behaviours – either to themselves or others. In practise this includes minimising, making excuses or justifying their words or actions, or explaining away these behaviours as anything other than what they are.

Let's consider the differences in the following examples between empathy and enabling.

Enabling looks and sounds like:

'You're right, the manager was too harsh. You're right, they are out of order. You don't need to change anything.'

'Don't worry, I'll handle your presentation, so you don't have to stress.'

'Let me talk to HR and explain why you couldn't meet the deadline.'

'I'll do it.'

Empathy looks and sounds more like care with boundaries.

'I can totally understand you're frustrated with the feedback.'

'It sounds like you're feeling overwhelmed at the moment – what do you think might be helpful?'

'I can see this situation is difficult for you.'

'What do you think your options are? What can you do?'

You can understand somebody's feelings without managing them for them or taking care of them or their responsibilities. It is important in addressing narcissistic abuse and toxicity in the workplace that we stop enabling it in any way.

Empathise with their emotions.

Don't enable their actions.

Set boundaries. Aim to hold narcissists at work accountable – either directly or through taking the necessary steps to escalate – and let the natural consequences unfold.

22

L – Log Interactions

Keeping a log of interactions with toxic people at work can be helpful in several ways. First of all, it can help with your own perspective and support your own processing to see events written down in black and white. It can be easy to lose perspective or struggle with memory when you're under stress, but keeping a log can help you to see the situation more clearly and from a more grounded, objective perspective. It may also, if issues progress, be an important record that you rely on at a later stage.

Documenting toxic interactions or examples of workplace bullying, harassment or abuse is essentially professional self-preservation.

Try to make a note of events or interactions as soon as possible after they happen. It is more useful to do this while the details are still fresh in your mind. Writing about this can also help you to process it to some degree.

Keep to objective facts. Try not to load any records with your emotions – although by all means journal about them for yourself elsewhere; that can be a useful and supportive way for you to work through your feelings.

For the purposes of professional record-keeping of interactions, try to be precise and factual.

For example, rather than recording, 'Louise was a complete nightmare on this project', record, 'Louise interrupted me eight times during my fifteen-minute presentation and aggressively said, "This is wrong", without providing any further feedback or opportunity for discussion. This was in front of five colleagues in the team. Some of whom mentioned afterwards they were also shocked by her rudeness and attitude.'

You can use the following 5Ws Framework to document interactions:

WHEN did it occur? (date, time, duration)

WHERE did this take place? (online, in the meeting room, etc.)

WHO was there? (the names of the people present)

WHAT exactly happened? (include direct quotes wherever possible)

WHY is this significant to document? (name what kind of abuse or harassment this is an example of where possible or why this was inappropriate)

Keep a log of any incidents of:

- verbal abuse including silent treatment or withholding of information, threats or intimidation, humiliation or belittling
- unreasonable demands or impossible-to-meet deadlines
- guilt-tripping, toxic gossiping or manipulation
- examples of sabotage or claiming the credit for your

work, or any other kinds of discriminatory comments or behaviour

Include specific incidents or interactions as well as any themes or patterns of behaviour you experience. For example, somebody repeatedly interrupting or undermining you; consistent or deliberate exclusion from important meetings or communications; interpersonal problem-causing behaviours, favouritism, lies or misleading information; examples of toxic communication patterns; repeated pushing of your boundaries; or regular deadline changes.

Keep this record on a personal device or email and back up with a physical notebook too. Don't solely use the company system, as the information can be accessed or deleted at any time. Keep your records separate from work.

Issues may or may not need to be escalated; however, either way, it is useful to have a record of key events. Your records are powerful as they can show:

- patterns of inappropriate or unfair behaviour
- any escalation of these behaviours
- the impact of this on you, your work, health, mental health or career progression
- whether there are any witnesses who will also corroborate what has occurred

Another effective way to document evidence can be to confirm discussions or requests via email to the other person. After verbal conversations, send a follow-up email with something along the lines of:

'Dear **[name]**, thanks for your time today. Further to our discussion I just wanted to confirm that you've asked me to **[name the request]** by **[deadline]**. I wanted to just clarify that **[add any concerns or details]**. Could you please confirm and let me know if I've misunderstood anything? Many thanks, I look forward to hearing from you.'

This kind of written email communication serves to confirm the conversation that was had and the request that was made, and it also nudges the other person to either confirm the unreasonable request in writing (in which case you have it evidenced) or to backtrack. Getting into the habit of doing this can be protective for you. It really doesn't matter how anybody else feels about it – remember, this kind of documentation is to protect you professionally.

If possible, draw on support from understanding, supportive colleagues here. If others in the company are also experiencing or witnessing harassment or abuse, it can be impactful to your case to record their statements too. You can encourage one another to log interactions, or take steps together to make formal complaints.

Keeping a record and documenting examples and patterns of toxic behaviour may not stop the narcissist behaving in the ways that narcissists do. However, it will help protect you if or when that behaviour or complaint needs to be reported or escalated. Do bear in mind, when you are documenting incidents, that, should things go further, HR departments and legal professionals tend to be more interested in reported incidents and patterns of workplace harassment or abuse than in feelings. Legal cases are built on evidence, not emotions.

Next let's go over delegating and deciding what to do next should things continue or worsen.

23

D – Delegate and Decide

Workplace toxicity and in particular narcissistic abuse is often very insidious. Like a lot of toxic relationships, the abuse tends to start small, before gradually increasing over time to the point where it is deeply impactful, damaging and unbearable. Narcissistic abuse is also the kind of psychological and emotional manipulation that leaves a person wondering if in fact they've got it wrong, or even if they are imagining it. If you are in this situation at the moment, you may wonder if you're being too sensitive or overreacting for considering escalating your concerns. If so, please know that questioning and second-guessing yourself in this way is in itself a symptom of this kind of abuse. Narcissistic abuse undermines your emotional experience and can cause you to lose trust in yourself. Always remember that your feelings matter and you can trust your judgement.

Escalating issues at work is an attempt to work towards or find some kind of resolution or solution to the issue. It is therefore an important and sometimes necessary part of the process, particularly when an individual or culture is having a negative impact on your or others' mental health, well-being and career.

Ideally, first steps are taken to address the issues with the individual. However, as we know, this is especially challenging when it comes to the narcissist at work as their rigid and manipulative interpersonal and communication style together with their lack of accountability makes it very difficult, if not impossible, to reason with them. When you cannot reason with someone it is right to take your issue to the relevant person and no longer try to manage or put up with it alone.

Raising concerns about a narcissistic colleague the same level as you or junior is often more straightforward than addressing the same concerns about more senior members of staff, depending on the set-up and policies of the organisation. And if you are in business with a narcissist then that dynamic needs to be navigated too.

I'm afraid the reality is that there are more challenges and limitations if the narcissism is coming from the top – or if you are in a business partnership with one. If that is the case, it likely means that the narcissistic toxicity is deeply ingrained in the culture of the organisation or set-up and the ripple effects will be felt throughout board level and management and will filter down. A strong culture of ruling through fear, control and manipulation is very difficult to change and it may be that deciding if it's the right environment for you is the more suitable step. If you are in a business partnership with a narcissist, it may be that you will need legal advice to find the best way to detach or separate. That generally means one of you leaving or finding a way to move forward with minimal contact.

Knowing when to escalate issues to management, HR, or to take legal advice, is a very individual choice. There may be several reasons to factor into your decision. Generally, red flag indicators for it being time to escalate include:

- A consistent pattern or culture of abuse. If you are experiencing or witnessing repeated instances of undermining, bullying, criticism, harassment or discriminatory behaviour, then it's time to escalate. One-off incidents can be addressed directly at the time, but patterns indicate systemic issues that really do need a formal intervention.
- When the narcissism and toxicity at work is having a negative impact on your mental health. Sure, sometimes a level of work-related stress is understandable, but in healthy environments it is short-lived and you generally feel supported – both at the time and longer-term – in terms of your well-being and professional goals.
- When it is causing you stress that affects your health, your ability to do your job, your relationships, sleep or overall well-being. Toxic environments compromise your physical health and well-being and that's a clear sign that escalating and addressing the actions is necessary.
- Any behaviour that violates company policies, employment or general law or safety. Any actions that create a hostile, toxic work environment should be reported and taken further.
- When protocols, professional or ethical guidelines are not being adhered to. Any risk to or safety concerns around colleagues or customers must be reported. Any discriminatory or inappropriate actions should be escalated.
- When you feel you cannot address the issues with the

person directly. This is not unusual with a narcissist, and it is absolutely right to escalate your concerns to somebody else – a more senior manager, a director or HR. It may also be necessary to take legal advice or consult any professional body or insurer for support and guidance.

It can be useful to follow a few guidelines to help with the escalation process. Firstly, as mentioned in the previous section, keep a log of interactions. Document as much as you can and get together any evidence or witnesses.

Follow proper channels. There may be a protocol for escalation within your organisation or union. Either way, start with the next person in line in a supervisory role who is not part of the problem. If that's not possible, go to HR, more senior management or, if needed, external bodies, unions or a solicitor. Try to focus on objective facts and actions as well as the impact the problem has had on you, the work environment, professional or team dynamics, company culture, your work performance or career progression. Remember: principles over personalities.

Taking steps towards escalation may offer you support and relief. Seek out additional support for yourself during this time, be it from friends or family or professionally – in either individual or group services. There can be a real power in speaking with others who have been through the same thing.

Jack was a very impressive young entrepreneur who created a start-up with a friend from university. He was very ambitious and had a bold and clear vision of what he wanted to build. He believed his friend and business partner would be an ideal match to take care of the sales and marketing side of things. While Jack and a team of developers worked hard to get the products ready, he trusted his partner was taking care of the work within his role and responsibility.

However, as the company progressed Jack started to realise that, not only was his business partner not doing much at all, he was mostly busy networking to brag and take full credit for the concept and company, for his own ego. Otherwise, he wasn't bringing much to the partnership or business at all. Not only that, but he also then started to cause issues within the team. He would say things to certain members of staff that created fears and worries about job security and the future of the business. This quickly worsened. He then attempted to create division and mistrust between the team and Jack. Fortunately, trust and loyalties had already been built and so Jack was made aware of this toxic disruption.

With no other management in place at this point, Jack had no option other than to seek external support for himself; from a psychologist and a business mentor, who both encouraged him to take legal steps to remove the toxic person from the business. This process wasn't without stress and upset, but with support Jack was able to focus on his key objective and his own self-care, while lawyers managed the steps to negotiate the other person's exit. A key part of this process for Jack was letting go of his own need to control the narrative. His business partner's narcissistic ego meant he needed to have his own self-promoting version of events – and as he exited he relayed his own story about why he'd left.

According to him, he had single-handedly developed the

business and was now bored – he was moving on to 'bigger and better' projects. He received a payout, which, while frustrating, was ultimately a small price to pay considering the further disruption and distress he could have caused if he stayed. Following his departure, harmony, focus and morale were immediately restored and the business went on to thrive.

Narcissists will always have their own version of events. It's freeing for you, as it was for Jack, to just let them. Jack knows the truth. You know the truth.

Narcissists try to rule through fear and guilt. They are power-hungry and will bully others using intimidation and a sense of holding power over your role or career. But please remember: what a narcissist threatens to do and what they will or even can actually do are more often than not entirely different things.

A key part of being able to take steps to escalation may include managing your own fear or guilt, which a narcissist for sure will have stirred up for their own advantage. Holding abusive people accountable for their actions is the right thing to do. Standing up to workplace bullies is a professional and appropriate step to take. Toxic people and work environments normalise inappropriate behaviour and make employees question their own perceptions.

Trust yourself and your instincts. If something feels wrong, then it probably is. Escalating issues isn't about causing trouble. It's about standing up for yourself and for what is right and this is intrinsically steered by your moral compass. It's about taking steps to create a healthier work environment for yourself and everyone else. We all deserve to work in an abuse-free space and one that supports professional growth and personal well-being. The more we stand up to narcissistic behaviour and abuse in the workplace, the more we can push this inappropriate and toxic culture out. In the meantime, you can focus on continuing to build any additional skills or qualifications you'd like to in order to further your career or personal development – in or beyond your current workplace. Continue to network within and outside the company. Narcissists prefer people to shrink, but at this point you can consider where and how else you can grow personally and professionally.

Deciding When Enough Is Enough

Escalation can lead to a resolution and help oust the most problematic narcissist or toxic people in the workplace so that an enjoyable, healthy work life can resume. Sometimes, however, for whatever reason this is not effective or possible. It is of course wrong to have to make a professional move due to a toxic person or culture. However, if this is having a very detrimental impact on you, your well-being or your career, then it is something to seriously consider. No job is worth your mental health or well-being. Viable options and exit strategies may include a change in role or department. You could start with considering alternative opportunities within the company. Or it may be that it's time for a new, external and different opportunity. It's a good time to actively network and explore options. It could even be the time and opportunity to completely reconsider your career.

When Sophie set up a business with a man she'd previously worked with and had known for many years, it was a dream come true. She put a lot of her personal finances into the partnership, not to mention the hours and hours of work and graft needed for the company launch. The vision was clear and the potential for the business growth and financial return was incredible.

However, a few months into setting up, Sophie's business partner started to become very difficult. He wasn't doing any work. He simply wasn't contributing like he had agreed to. He had close connections to their main investor and at the same time he started to complain to them that it was Sophie who wasn't contributing and making things difficult.

It quickly got to the point where the partner was blocking every step forward and making even the simplest of decisions difficult. He would be confrontational and at times aggressive. Once Sophie lost her temper and showed her frustration, and of course her abusive narcissistic business partner immediately jumped on that as 'proof' that Sophie was the problem, was emotionally unstable and needed to leave.

Sophie's dream was fast becoming a complete nightmare. She started having difficulty sleeping, feeling anxious and panicky, and was experiencing serious signs of stress including heart palpitations and dizzy spells. It was a painful process of realisation and coming to terms with the fact she was now in a financial and business bind with somebody so toxic and abusive. The triangulation between the business partner and the main investor meant that that dynamic really was an engineered 'us' versus her. The narcissist here was typically controlling and pocketing communication, being sure to be the middleman and so blocking any direct communication between Sophie and the investor. At the same time, he was making out that she was untrustworthy and mentally ill.

Her position quickly became very limited and isolated. With the extent to which the manipulation and stress were affecting her health and mental health, Sophie ultimately felt she had to step away from the business. As she experienced shock, anger, grief and letting go, she was forced to make a decision about what was best for her. As part of this she had to reflect on what really mattered to her and, while financial success and status were important to her, she ultimately valued her health and well-being more. Sophie left, and took time to process the trauma of what she had been through. She re-evaluated her priorities and focused on what really mattered in life – her well-being and happiness. Within a few years she had moved on and set up her own successful well-being business.

In order to reach a decision regarding when enough is enough, it can be useful to revisit the exercises from earlier on in this book on evaluating your morals and values. Consider what your priorities are, at this stage, in work and in your life.

What matters most and least to you?

What do you want in the immediate, short and longer term?

Is the role or current situation aligned with this?

What impact is it having on your life?

On your mental health and well-being?

Is it taking a negative toll on your relationships?

How much work/life balance do you have?

Are you holding out in the hope or fantasy that things might change or be different?

What are the benefits of staying versus leaving?

What is the reality of the situation?

It is important to take a grounded inventory on the current situation. Earlier we looked at identifying your key values, as our boundaries are shaped by them. Take some time to reflect on how supportive your values are to you and your goals. Some values can leave us more vulnerable to putting up with abuse or persevering in toxic work situations. I've worked with many clients over the years who were deeply unhappy and negatively impacted by working in toxic cultures under narcissistic bully-bosses with really awful behaviours and treatment – the sorts of bosses who would time their toilet breaks and constantly undermine them in every possible way, day in, day out. It's impossible to not be negatively impacted by that. However, for some, their priority at that time was largely financial. Their values reflected that. And so they would desperately try to push on against the odds, with tunnel vision, to reach their financial goals, even if it meant being subjected to workplace toxicity and having their self-esteem and confidence battered – not to mention the impact of the stress on their physical and mental health. This can only realistically be done for so long.

Logically, personally, I think there is no point in accumulating financial wealth if you no longer have the physical or mental health to enjoy it. But it is what some people choose to tolerate for a period of time, in order to reach their end goal – that end goal actually being reflective of their values and what's important to them. It's not for me, or anyone else, to judge a person's values or choices, or what is most important to you at any given point in life. However, I would urge you to consider and reflect on what your values are, and why and specifically whether they are a vulnerability or a strength for you.

Our values can change. It's natural for our priorities to change throughout our lives; what drives us in our twenties can be different to what drives us in our forties or fifties or in later life. Sometimes experiencing abuse and toxicity at work can be the very catalyst we need to make us reflect on what matters or what we really want and desire. Staying current and close to your personal values really help you to be clearer in yourself about your boundaries, wants, needs and what matters. This in turn makes your decisions much easier.

Reflect fearlessly and honestly on what really matters most and least to you at this point – both professionally and personally – and trust that the right path will become clear. What kind of work environment would be the best fit for your values now?

You can use the GROW model to help navigate your decision:

G – Goal What do you want to achieve?

R – Reality What is happening now?

O – Options What are your options? What could you do?

W – Way forward What will you do? What is the right choice for you?

One thing I will share, for sure, that I personally believe is always the case, and I've witnessed in my own professional and personal experience – **people always ultimately feel better for leaving a toxic relationship**. Of any kind.

Being subjected to narcissistic abuse very much leaves a person feeling like they are stuck, trapped, that they can't trust themselves, they are scared, confused and that their self-esteem and confidence have been seriously knocked. These feelings are in themselves symptoms of being in a toxic relationship. I can honestly share that, in every case I've ever seen, when people get away from narcissistic abuse they find they are quickly restored to a more balanced sense of perspective and peace. Sometimes, it's just finding the strength to take that step.

Next, I'd like to share more about the journey of taking that step and some thoughts and ideas about moving forward.

PART FOUR:
MOVING FORWARD

24

Protecting Yourself and Your Organisation

Dealing with difficult and toxic people at work may be unavoidable at times – to a degree it is a part of work life. But toxic cultures and patterns of abusive behaviour are a serious problem. You can protect yourself from workplace toxicity moving forward by spotting the signs and implementing the ideas and actions that we've covered.

Being informed about and learning how to recognise narcissism and narcissists at work, and the ripple effects of this in individuals and organisations, is key. There may be indicators you can look out for during the interview stage. Sometimes it may be hidden and only start to emerge later on, or somebody might come into the organisation after you and disrupt the vibe. Anyway, knowing what workplace toxicity is and how to spot it also gives you a shift in perspective when you can view and understand the abuse for what it is – reflective of that person's issues. It's not you or your fault. There are just people like that out there. Odds are you will come into contact with at least one at some point in your working life. When you adopt the grounded and balanced perspective that the other person is the problem, you will be much more able to hold them appropriately to account – and take the necessary steps to involve others and address the issues.

Developing your own personal toolbox of emotional regulation and self-care techniques is vitally important for your own mental health and well-being. As is setting and maintaining boundaries – in both your professional and personal life.

Maintaining work/life balance requires good boundaries, care and discipline.

As we've discussed, if needed, work on any issues that get in the way of you feeling comfortable setting and holding appropriate boundaries with people at work or in relation to managing appropriate work/life availability and demands. Boundaries are crucial to protect our well-being and relationships. Managing stress is an ongoing practice – keep an eye on your stress levels on a regular basis. Make regular time for exercise and play and activities that rest and restore your nervous system. Seek support from trusted colleagues, professionals, friends or family.

Define what is acceptable for yourself as an individual and for others in the organisation, including what is acceptable behaviour and communication. A healthy workplace environment is one where there is open, direct and clear communication. It's a place where people feel safe to share their thoughts, feelings or ideas, knowing there won't be any judgement or criticism. Foster that in yourself, your team and the wider workplace.

If we all highlight every time toxic communication occurs, it leaves little room for it.

There should be a zero-tolerance policy for bullying and harassment. This means standing up and speaking out any time you experience or witness them. Check that your company has proper policies in place and, if it doesn't, consider if this is something you can arrange or request. Regular training on recognising toxic behaviours and/or healthy boundaries, effective communication and supportive psychological practices in work is a good idea for any company that values its people and culture.

If you are in a management, leadership or human resources type role, encourage open dialogue about any workplace or interpersonal issues and be supportive to anyone who reports them, creating multiple channels for feedback and complaints. Clarity around company vision and values related to this and adherence to them really help support a safe and supportive work environment.

Limiting power dynamics between people at work can help eliminate a platform for abusers. Open and transparent ways of working, including discussions, clear role definition, clarity around responsibilities and effective communication, can make it difficult, if not impossible, for toxic, narcissistic people to operate. Healthy practices will make them stand out. A healthy work environment is a place where they will not fit in. This will be very apparent, and they usually don't stick around to be shamed for it.

Practise ethical decision making – even if or when it's difficult. More often than not, narcissistic people move on to whoever and wherever they can get their much-needed supply of admiration, attention, power and control. One of the best things you can do to protect yourself now and in the future is to be sure that person is not you and that your workplace is not the platform for them or people like them.

Interviews

Getting away from a toxic work environment is one of the most common reasons a person voluntarily resigns from a job, irrespective of industry. This is no surprise: being in a toxic, bullying culture at work, where there are troublesome dynamics, poor communication, low morale, lack of appropriate boundaries, mistrust, deceit and so on, is obviously so detrimental to one's well-being.

It's always a great decision to leave any kind of situation or relationship that is negatively impacting your mental health, if possible. But if you have done this and moved on, how do you explain this at subsequent interviews? And what can you do to minimise the risk of finding yourself in that kind of workplace again?

A really helpful exercise to do as preparation for any future job changes is to take some time to reflect on what matters most and least to you at work. Take some time to consider:

What do you enjoy and detest at work?

What do you feel like you've learnt and would change from your previous experience?

What helps you thrive?

Are you a team player or would you prefer to work more independently?

What would you prefer to never have to do again?

The clearer you are about what you like and what works for you and what doesn't, the easier it will be to explain this to others and to assess for it during the interview process.

Remember: the interview process works two ways. The reality is that most people have experienced some form of negative toxicity at work at some point, whether directly or through witnessing others going through it. Most people can relate to it. Therefore, I don't think this is something that you should be concerned or scared about discussing. If anything, having an open, upfront conversation about it can be incredibly helpful for both parties. It helps your interviewers understand your experience and motivations and it can also help you to understand their values and ethos on the matter. Honesty and transparency are generally the healthiest and best policy all round.

How much detail you go into about your experience, though, is entirely up to you. However, I would suggest that, in the spirit of professionalism, you aim to go with an explanation that is authentic yet succinct.

Having enough personal and professional support to be able to share, vent and process what you've previously experienced can help you to feel more prepared and ready to start afresh in a new role and to discuss it with more ease.

1 *Prepare a Brief Explanation*

Consider how and what you'd like to share about your previous workplace. I suggest not getting into too much detail, but explaining enough so that your interviewers can get to know more about you and your motivations. For example, you might explain that you didn't feel that the previous work environment was a match in terms of values, views or vision. You prefer a flat management structure, more transparent communication, support for training and development or structure – or whatever it is that you would like in a new role. Be clear about what you'd like to be different – in a positive way. Share your thoughts about what a role, company or work environment would ideally be like for you for a long-term mutually rewarding future.

2 *Keep It Real*

Inauthenticity is communicated in what you say and how you say it. Being too vague or cagey could come across as dishonest and may raise a sense of mistrust. This is one of the reasons why it's important to prepare an explanation and to try to be as clear and transparent as feels comfortable for you. Being open and honest invites others to do the same, and any interview based on all sides being transparent and real is a successful interview, regardless of the outcome.

Ideally, it's best to be grounded and real about your capabilities and what you are looking for, as well as the role and what the organisation are realistically seeking, expecting and suited to. This is a key part of avoiding, as best as is possible, finding yourself in a workplace situation that is not right for you or vice versa.

There is little point in having hopes and fantasies about what the people or role *could* be. It's much more beneficial to keep it real and discuss and understand the reality of it so all parties can make a grounded assessment of suitability all round. Remember: this works both ways.

3 Be Positive

If at all possible, balance a brief and honest explanation about the previous toxic work culture or person with some positives. Again, this comes from your reflections on what you can take from what you've been through and what you'd honestly like – and not like – moving forward.

Going through workplace abuse and bullying is a truly awful and unfair experience, yet at the same time it almost always ultimately brings about some degree of post-traumatic growth; it was a difficult time, but you can come away from it feeling clearer about yourself and your values, with a renewed sense of purpose, strength and gratitude.

At interview, you might share some examples of what you've learnt or come to realise from your previous difficult experience. For example:

'My last role really highlighted to me my desire to ...

... work in a supportive team environment.

... work more independently.

... work in an environment where effective communication and personal development is encouraged and supported.'

'My previous employer didn't offer any training or progression and I'd actually like to learn more and work in a place where development is supported.'

Other Considerations

Ask questions. Be sure to ask enough questions so that you feel confident enough in your understanding of the role, the expectations and the environment.

Some ideas for useful questions include:

- *Is there a typical work day?* If so, what does that look like? If not, what can you expect?
- *What is the background of the business?* This can help you to understand the nature of how the company has grown; whether there has been organic or aggressive growth. *How long have they (the interviewers) been there?* What are staff retention rates? This can be very telling about the culture.
- *What have their professional journeys been?* Have they progressed in the business to their current role? Or was it entry-level?
- *How flexible are aspects of the role/hours/work location etc., if at all?*
- *Do people tend to keep to the same work hours?* It can be helpful to get some insight into the attitudes around start and finish times, as well as overtime and how this is viewed.
- *What opportunities are there for training and skills or*

career progression? What is the company's viewpoint on this?

- *How would you describe the working culture of the organisation?* Simply asking them directly is a great way to gauge a sense of this. Again, it invites an opportunity for a transparent discussion so you can both assess the fit.
- *Can you tell me more about the team I'll be working with?* This question can help you understand more about the structure, and the way it is described can offer useful insight.
- *Is this a new role or replacing somebody who has left?* If the latter, explore why the person has left/is leaving. What potential positives or negatives do they foresee about this?
- *What is the performance review process like?*
- *What attributes do you think it takes to be successful in this role/company?*
- *What are the company's most important values and vision?* This is very telling as to what matters most to the company and if that is a clear, shared vision. It is also helpful to understand more about the interviewers' views on this.
- *What is the leadership style here?*
- *Can you describe the work environment and culture here?*

Explain what you'd ideally like, in both the short and long term. Be confident about being clear and transparent on this. They can reciprocate.

There are no rights or wrongs as such. It's more about understanding and assessing for the organisations set-up, views, values, expectations and preferences in comparison to your own.

Assessing for Narcissism

While conducting a full-on clinical assessment is probably not possible at interview (or any) stage, you can look out for some telltale warning signs and red flags for narcissism when being interviewed by potential employers (or interviewing others for a position at your place of work).

Red flags for narcissism during the interview process (both ways) include:

- A focus on one's own individual achievement while dismissing others' contributions. This could come from either the interviewer or interviewee. Look out for how they describe their professional successes. Is it a balanced combination of individual and team work or the *me, me, me* show?
- Acknowledgements of help, contributions, teamwork or support from others that seem like a box-ticking, insincere gesture.
- Inauthentic platitudes of any kind.
- Inflated sense of self-importance. You may get the sense they are exaggerating achievements or qualifications. They may be misleading about them.
- Lack of genuine empathy or compassion. Discussing

relationships at work can reveal any difficulties with understanding, sharing or caring about the feelings of others. Does this feel like genuine or cognitive empathy?

- Dominating or controlling the conversation excessively and without seeming self-aware about doing so.
- Not asking questions. Not wanting to get to know or understand others or the set-up.
- Lack of listening. Interrupting. Repeatedly and predominantly talking about themselves beyond what is being asked.
- Displaying arrogance or haughtiness. Thinking they already know all the answers. Note also how they speak to other staff members or greet reception, security etc.

If you are the one being interviewed, note how the interviewing panel appear to get on and interact between themselves.

Setting a group task to complete as part of the interview process can also be a great way to see how a person interacts and works with others. It can be helpful to see if a person can work harmoniously with a group, whether they are more of a leader or if they just operate as a team of one.

Inviting an opportunity for feedback or reflection can be informative. Narcissistic people struggle with criticism and self-reflection. Offering constructive criticism can be a helpful way to spot signs.

Offer some relevant constructive criticism and watch for how a person reacts. Narcissists don't react well to criticism at all. Look out for a defensive reaction, perhaps irritation or annoyance, even anger, even if it's for just a second. Manipulative narcissists may then try to cover it well with politeness – but you may see that it's through gritted teeth.

Also, offering an opportunity to reflect on a set task or even the interview itself can be a helpful way to assess a person's ability to reflect on a shared experience. Are their reflections fair and considerate, balanced and accurate? Or skewed and distorted?

What is your sense of their values? What appears to be most important to them? Money, fame, power and accolades may be red flags.

What is their definition of success? Is it focused on superficial or selfish gains, or genuinely for the good of their people or organisation? Is it a match with yours or your organisations?

Importantly, notice how are you left feeling following this meeting or interaction. Extremes of any kind may be a warning sign. As is finding yourself thinking excessively about them – I find this can be an indicator of how much attention a person commands.

Further Reflections

Take time during interviews to consider both the content and the process. They are both equally important, in my opinion. That is, consider what has been discussed and how it's been communicated. Consider, honestly and objectively, what has been said and what has been your experience throughout the whole process.

Above all, trust your gut. If something feels too good to be true – it's probably because it is. If something doesn't feel right, or you find yourself troubled by something you're sensing, trust that.

Trust yourself and your instincts.

25

Protecting Yourself and Your Career

Congratulations on moving on, whether that be the removal of the narcissistic toxic person at work, leaving your department or deciding enough is enough and moving to somewhere new. This can mark an exciting step for positive change and for never again having to deal with anything so toxic at work. In order for you to continue to grow from your experience, possibly armed with new information, insight and tools, there are a number of steps and practices that can help protect you, your well-being and your career hereon in. They are:

- Protect and take good care of yourself by maintaining an overall healthy work/life balance.
- Make time for regular physical activity and exercise. It is one of the most important things you can do for your mental health and for managing stress – not to mention your physical fitness. It's usually one of the first things to go when we get stressed too. Make it a priority.

- Take regular breaks to decompress. Book these in advance so you have them in the diary. Stick to them.
- Start each work day with positive intentions and boundaries in mind.
- Repeat self-soothing or confidence, self-esteem boosting 'I statements', e.g. 'I am good enough', 'I deserve balance and respect', 'I am a good person', 'It's OK to rest'.
- Practise deep breathing and mindfulness practices. Make this a regular part of your day.
- End your work day with a clear transition ritual to mark work to home. This may be the commute home; or, if you're working from home, take a walk when you finish for the day, and leave work at work.
- Make time for hobbies or interests outside of work. Protect this.
- Make time for and maintain healthy relationships outside of work.
- Consider professional or specialist support or counselling if stress or other issues become too challenging or overwhelming or you have symptoms of trauma or PTSD. Know that seeking support is a strength.
- Set and hold healthy boundaries around work hours. Switch-off time from work is essential for our well-being. Start as you mean to go on, but review this and readjust whenever you need to.
- Keep practising and developing your boundary-setting skills.
- Regularly check in and reflect on your professional life – recognise any early warning signs of potential issues so

you can take steps to address them before they escalate.

- Remember that other people's issues are their responsibility. Your responsibility is you and your boundaries.
- Take time to celebrate your contributions and achievements.
- Remind yourself of what you do well.
- Focus on your professional goals and growth and maintain a healthy balance that is right for you.
- Focus on the positives and what there is to be grateful for currently.
- Enjoy it.

Remember: healthy workplaces do exist, and they support your growth and well-being. While you may need to navigate challenging personalities from time to time, your boundaries should be respected and inappropriate behaviour should be called out and people held to account. Setting boundaries with narcissists at work isn't just about managing the current situation, it's about developing skills and self-esteem that will serve you for your entire career and life – both in and out of work.

Trust your instincts – always.

You can both maintain professionalism and not put up with crap you don't need or want to. Please never hesitate to seek support when needed. And remember, you are worthy and deserve respect, success and happiness.

You cannot change a narcissist or difficult people at work,

but you can control your responses and make choices about how much involvement, if any, you have with them and how much you let them affect you.

A Journey from Workplace Toxicity to Healing

For three years, I walked into an office that slowly chipped away at my self-esteem and sense of self. What started as my dream job became a nightmare wrapped in professional language and corporate policies that somehow made the abuse feel justified and legitimate.

My manager, Mark, had a gift for making me question my own reality. 'I'm only trying to help you improve,' he'd say after publicly humiliating me in meetings. 'You're too sensitive' became his favourite phrase whenever I tried to address his behaviour. It would both shut me up and shut me down. The gaslighting was so subtle, so expertly woven into daily interactions, that I began to believe I was the problem. I can see this more clearly in hindsight.

The toxicity wasn't just Mark. The entire culture was infected. Colleagues who once smiled and chatted became distant, afraid to associate with someone who had fallen from grace. The office had an unspoken hierarchy of favourites and scapegoats. While I had started as a favourite, I had somehow then landed firmly in the latter category.

I started having panic attacks on Sunday nights. My stomach would knot at the thought of Monday morning. I'd lie awake rehearsing conversations, trying to predict which version of Mark I'd encounter – the charming one who praised me in front of senior management, or the cold one who nitpicked every email I sent.

The breaking point came during a team meeting when Mark criticised a project I'd worked on for weeks, dismissing months of effort with a casual, 'This isn't what we discussed.' Fortunately I had the emails. I had the notes. I knew I was right, yet, somehow, I found myself apologising and still promising to 'do better'.

That night, I called my sister and broke down completely. 'I don't recognise myself any more,' I sobbed. 'I used to be confident, capable. Now I second-guess everything I do.'

The decision to leave wasn't easy. The job market was tough, and part of me had internalised Mark's narrative that I was inadequate. But with the support of a therapist who specialised in workplace trauma, I began to see the situation clearly for the first time.

Recovery didn't happen overnight. Even after leaving, I carried the toxicity with me like invisible scars. At my new job I'd freeze up in meetings, waiting for the criticism that never came. I over-prepared for everything, terrified of being caught off-guard again.

Slowly, with patience and self-compassion, I began to rebuild. I learnt to recognise the difference between constructive feedback and psychological manipulation. I practised setting boundaries – something I'd never needed to do before that toxic environment taught me their importance.

The healing came in waves. Some days I felt strong and clear about what I'd endured. Other days, I'd catch myself wondering if maybe I had been too sensitive, if maybe Mark *was right. But each time, I'd remind myself of the truth: no one deserves to have their reality questioned, their confidence systematically dismantled, or have their worth tied to someone else's pathological need for control.*

Today, I work in an environment where respect is the baseline, not the exception. I've learnt to trust my instincts again, to speak up when something doesn't feel right. Most importantly, I've learnt that healing from workplace toxicity isn't just about finding a new job – it's about reclaiming the parts of yourself that were slowly eroded by someone else's toxicity and dysfunction.

If you're reading this and recognising your own experience, please know: it's not you. It was never you. You deserve to work in an environment where you are respected, where your contributions are valued, and where your voice matters.

The person you were before the toxicity? They're still there, waiting for you to remember who you are. Only now, from here on in, with even more awareness and strength gained from the experience.

26

Healing, Growth and Recovery

Toxic workplace experiences can leave wounds that cut into your sense of worth, self-esteem and identity. While you can develop boundaries and self-care and work on effective communication, it is difficult to fully heal while you remain in a toxic work environment. While around such dysfunction and sickness, a part of you will still be actively operating in some degree of survival mode. The primary function will be about getting through the days and weeks. There really is only so long any one of us can do this for before it takes a serious toll on our well-being. We either takes steps through delegating and escalating issues to remove the toxic person, or we make a decision to leave and move on. Only once the threat has passed can our nervous system start to more fully settle and recover.

If you're coming out of a toxic work environment, it's not just about moving on to another job – it's about healing and change.

This requires that we acknowledge the pain and the loss and give ourselves the time and tools to support our recovery.

A part of healing very much mirrors grieving. It's not just leaving a job; you can be mourning the loss, the lost trust, betrayal, dashed hopes or unmet potential. You may even be grieving a version of yourself that once felt confident and safe. Often people I work with talk about there being a distinct sense of 'before and after' narcissistic abuse in their lives. The experience changes you.

It is important to name what you've experienced and been through. Trauma doesn't necessarily always have to come from major catastrophic events. It can also come from chronic, low-grade stress that takes a toll on your nervous system over time. Narcissists at work bring with them a unique kind of relational traumatic impact – from the lies, the deceit, the betrayal, the passive-aggressiveness, the gaslighting, the punishing silences, intimidation and degree of manipulation. A key step in healing from this is to acknowledge:

This is not normal. It is not healthy. It is not OK. This harms me. It will come to an end. I will move on.

Acknowledging what has happened, being clear about what and who that person or people or culture are or were and the impact it's had on you is not weakness. It's vital clarity. Recognising and naming it for what it is, or was, is an important step in your recovery. Narcissists at work and toxic cultures dysregulate your nervous system. They trigger stress, anxiety and depression and really affect your sense of safety and sanity. Narcissists at work will try to convince you that you were the problem. You weren't and you aren't.

The Grief Process

There is a process of grief that follows the end of a toxic relationship or situation, or following a significant change. You may find that you grieve the time and effort you put into the role or into trying to make it work. You may grieve the loss or the change, as well as the hopes and dreams of what could have been.

There are stages of grief and change that you may recognise and work through. They are not necessarily linear, and in reality I think it can feel a little like two steps forward and two steps back at times, but in time you will see you do move forward and through your grief until you reach a place of acceptance and peace.

The stages of grief and adapting to change include:

Denial: The stage where you can't quite believe or don't want to believe this is happening. 'Oh, it's not that bad', 'Things will get better', 'They are nice really'.

Anger: As the reality sinks in, you feel aggrieved, irritated and angry. 'Why did they do this?' 'How could they get away with it?', 'Why didn't anybody do anything?'

Bargaining: This is the stage of wrestling with what else you might have done, or how things could have been different. 'If I'd just worked harder, maybe it would've changed', 'Maybe I should never have said anything and it would have just been fine'.

Depression: As you move through the stages of grief you will feel down and depressed. This is the part of the process where you connect with the impact of what you've been through. It can be a difficult stage and being kind and compassionate to yourself is especially important here.

Acceptance: Having worked through the other stages of change and grief, you will finally arrive at a place of reflection and acceptance. This is where the pain lifts and you can emerge with a renewed sense of awareness, purpose and strength to continue to build from. 'It happened. It hurt. And I'm still here.' 'I feel clearer about what I want and what is right now.'

This process doesn't have a set timescale and there is no rush. It's important that you give yourself space and time for each stage and emotion that you experience. As we touched on in the mindfulness exercises, being aware of your inner self-talk is important, especially through the stages of grief and change. Cultivating a kind and supportive internal relationship to yourself, your experience and your feelings is crucial – and in itself a part of the transformative healing.

Healing the Nervous System

Healing also includes helping to settle and rebuild a sense of safety, in your body and with others. Chronic workplace stress and emotional abuse will put you in survival mode. Your nervous system will be in a more or less constant state of fight, flight or freeze. Even after you leave the job, you may find you are still reacting or feeling on edge. It can take time for this to shift and settle. Some supportive body-based practices, which are wonderful to do regularly, are things like:

- mindful walking, walks in nature
- breathwork – slow breathing techniques, deep belly breaths

- journaling – writing about what's happened and how you feel emotionally and physically to help support your recovery and healing process
- movement with rhythm – walking, running, swimming, cycling, yoga
- body-based practices – such as yoga, tai chi, Pilates
- shaking or dancing – trauma and tension release exercises (TRE) or dance

Psychotherapy

Seeking specialist support and speaking with a qualified professional can be especially helpful. Talking therapy can be a wonderful support and really aid your process by providing you with a safe space to share and talk through what you've been through. There are specialist and specific trauma therapy approaches that can be especially beneficial for the unique experience of dealing with and recovering from narcissistic abuse. I highly recommend two approaches in particular:

EMDR Therapy

Eye movement desensitisation and reprocessing (EMDR) is a powerful, evidence-based therapeutic technique that helps you to process and heal from traumatic and distressing, stressful experiences. It can also help you to process grief, betrayal and relational trauma.

During an EMDR session, the therapist will guide you to focus on the distressing time or emotion while engaging in a form of bilateral stimulation, which can be through eye movements or tapping. This technique essentially enable your mind to process what you've been through more fully. It helps you to work through your thoughts and feelings about it all and subsequently alleviate the symptoms of trauma or PTSD.

EMDR therapy is especially useful if you are experiencing flashbacks, nightmares, intrusive or ruminating thoughts or feelings about what you've been through, or if you are finding you are struggling to move on from an aspect of your experience of workplace toxicity. Finding yourself triggered or activated in response to anything happening specifically at work is usually a good indicator of something that EMDR would be helpful with. For example, feeling jumpy or anxious when you see an email appear in your inbox or are called to a meeting.

You can find a list of trained EMDR therapists online through EMDR Association and psychologist directories.

Sensorimotor Psychotherapy

Sensorimotor psychotherapy is a body-orientated therapeutic approach that recognises that emotional distress and trauma is held in our bodies. It integrates a blend of talk therapy, mindful awareness of bodily sensations and movement to help you to process and heal from stress and trauma. Sensorimotor psychotherapy helps you to be aware and conscious of the mind/body connection and bodily responses and to help regulate the nervous system. You can find a register of sensorimotor psychotherapists on the institute's website.

Reclaiming Your Self-Esteem and Sense of Worth

Narcissists at work, in their manipulation and abuse, will distort a person's perception. You may have heard:

'You don't fit in.' (By the way, if you don't fit into a toxic set-up please know that is a very good thing!)

'You're being too sensitive.'

'It's you, you're not a team player.'

'You should just be grateful to have a job here.'

These sorts of messages are distortions and lies; manipulations designed to keep a person small and compliant.

Another key part of healing is reclaiming your truth – in terms of who you are both in and out of work.

Remind yourself what you are good at. What your skills and qualities are. What your strengths and characteristics are.

To reclaim your confidence, spend some time reflecting on:

Who was I before this job?

What did I love about myself before this experience?

What parts of myself do I want to rebuild or protect now?

What am I good at?

What do I enjoy?

What are my unique skills and attributes?

What positive feedback have I received?

Journal about this and write a bit each day to help rebuild your sense of worth and esteem. Perhaps ask healthy colleagues or friends and take on board positive feedback from them.

Daily affirmations can also support this:

'I am a good person.'

'I deserve to be heard.'

'It's OK to rest.'

'I am worthy.'

'I am grateful for my journey.'

Finding Meaning in Recovery

Post-traumatic growth (PTG) is the positive psychological trans-formation that occurs after a traumatic or difficult time, and it's something that I see happening an awful lot following narcissistic abuse. While such abuse is an incredibly difficult experience to go through, in all sorts of ways, it also brings with it an opportunity for growth and learning. I know for me, experiencing narcis-sistic abuse both personally and professionally meant I had to learn about toxic dynamics, codependency recovery, boundaries, effective communication and self-care. Working on the relation-ship with oneself is an inside job. Knowing yourself and your boundaries is key to protecting yourself from toxic people and behaviours. Through the most difficult times of narcissistic abuse at work, where my own dreams turned into a living nightmare, I was forced to have to really consider what was important to me. I had to re-evaluate a lot – and I'm glad I did. My understanding and focus shifted in terms of knowing what really matters to me in life.

What can you take from your experience? You may find your healing brings you **clarity**, **resilience** or **purpose**. Your experi-ences may lead you to be clearer about what you want and don't want, how you relate to others or how to be clearer about the kind of colleague or leader or person you want to be. You may find that you move forward with new or renewed insight and the wisdom of what you will never tolerate or accept again. You can do things differently from now, having learnt from what you've been through. It may be that your values shift and you put more emphasis on a healthy life balance. It may be that the experience has forced you to acknowledge and address what you needed to for the better. Although that can be painful at times, it's ultimately positive growth.

Gratitude

When you are in the midst of dealing with toxic behaviour it's easy to feel consumed with what went wrong. It may seem strange to try to consider what you might be grateful for at the time, but it can be a very helpful and powerful practice that supports your healing and recovery.

Gratitude isn't about pretending everything was OK. It's about finding the small lights that helped you to get through this, or helped you to grow, even in the darkness.

I'm not suggesting being grateful for the abusive or toxic experience. I'm suggesting honouring what helped you through and what gains you have from getting through this (because you will get through it, and maybe already have!).

Take some time to journal and reflect on:

What helped me get through this?

Who supported me through this?

What skills or insight have I gained here?

What part of myself can I be grateful for or proud of?

What new boundaries do I have now that I appreciate?

What moments of peace or relief do I experience?

A powerful recovery practice is writing a gratitude list at the end of each day, where you reflect on:

What am I grateful for today?

Write down as many things as you can think of – no matter how big or small – and keep adding to it.

You Are Not Alone

Narcissists at work can be found anywhere and everywhere – regardless of the amount of hours worked, the level of position or sector. They may be overt or covert types, or maybe even a mixture. Workplace toxicity is common; it is something I believe most, if not all of us will experience at one point or another in our careers, to varying degrees. It is not your fault. They just exist. It's not for you to try to change or control that, or them. You can only control or change what you do. The shift in focus in itself marks the path of growth.

There is growth, healing and recovery to be gained from this experience. You are not 'too much' or 'too sensitive'. You are human. And you are healing.

Please remember: you deserve to feel safe, respected and valued – at work and beyond. We all do.

Your healing and growth is your own individual journey. I truly hope that some of the information and ideas I've shared here with you help you along the way. And I wish you all the very best in navigating any difficult situation you are currently facing and in your growth, healing and moving on from your experience with narcissism at work.

APPENDIX

QUIZ
Is This a Narcissist at Work?

1. Do they constantly seek attention and admiration? Even for the smallest of tasks or non-work-related matters?
2. Do they regularly talk or brag or name-drop about their own accomplishments, contacts or status?
3. Do they unfairly take credit for your or the team's work, and not give credit where it's due?
4. Do they lack empathy, understanding or compassion when you or others are struggling?
5. What happens if/when a mistake is made at work? Are they quick to react defensively? Are they quick to blame and shame others and/or not reflect on their own behaviours? Do they refuse to accept any responsibility?
6. Do they expect special treatment or behave as if they are more important than anyone else?
7. Do they react badly to any criticism – even if it's constructive?
8. Do they push or not respect other people's boundaries, i.e. not respect people's time – contact people when they're off sick or on leave?

9. Do they manipulate others through fear or guilt-tripping in order to get what they want?

10. Do they try to surround themselves with people who protect, enable or flatter them?

11. Are they obsessed with their image, reputation or how people see them?

12. Are they charming and persuasive at times, only to be then demeaning, controlling and punitive as and when it serves them?

13. Do they only seem to have superficial or fairly short-lived relationships professionally and/or personally?

14. Are they arrogant, haughty or rude?

15. Do they tend to like the sound of their own voice and dominate and talk over others in meetings?

16. Do they appear envious of your or others' success or achievements?

17. Do they try to pit colleagues against one another to create a competitive, mistrusting, unsupportive work environment?

18. Do they exaggerate, mislead or lie about their skills, experience or connections in order to appear more important or elite?

19. Do they seem to view relationships as transactional, only 'helping' others if there's something to gain for themselves?

20. Do you feel stressed, anxious, 'less than' or drained following interactions with them?

While this isn't a diagnostic tool, these twenty statements give you an idea of the themes of narcissism at work. The higher the score, the more likely it is that this individual is a narcissist.

References and Further Reading

Narcissism: Origins, Prevalence and Impact

Azazz, A.M.S. (2024). 'Amplifying Unheard Voices or Fueling Conflict? Exploring the dual-edged influence of leader narcissism in the hospitality industry.' *Administrative Sciences*, 14(12), 344. MDPI.

Bernerth, J.B. (2022). 'Does the Narcissist (and Those Around Him/Her) Pay a Price for Being Narcissistic? An Empirical Study of Leaders' Narcissism and Well-Being.' *Journal of Business Ethics*, 177, 533–46.

Biolik, E. (2025). 'Different shades of narcissism at work: The relationships of narcissism dimensions with work-related outcomes. *Personality and Individual Differences*.

Böhm, F. (2025). '"I can't get no satisfaction!" The critical role of political skill for workplace status and career satisfaction in grandiose narcissism.' *Acta Psychologica*.

Brummelman, E., Thomaes, S., Nelemans, S.A., Orobio de Castro, B., Overbeek, G. & Bushman, B.J. (2015). 'Origins of narcissism in children.' *Proceedings of the National Academy of Sciences*, 112(12), 3659–62.

Dhawan, N., Kunik, M.E., Oldham, J. & Coverdale, J. (2009). 'Prevalence and treatment of narcissistic personality disorder in the community: a systematic review.' *Comprehensive Psychiatry*, 51(4), 333–39.

Gebauer, J., Sedikides, C., Verplanken, B. & Maio, G. (2012). 'Communal Narcissism.' *Journal of Personality and Social Psychology*, 103(5), 854–78.

Luo, Y.L.L. & Cai, H. (2018). 'The Etiology of Narcissism: A Review of Behavioral Genetic Studies'. In: Hermann, A., Brunell, A., Foster, J. (eds) *Handbook of Trait Narcissism*. Springer.

Luo, Y.L.L., Cai, H. & Song, H. (2014). 'A Behavioral Genetic Study on Intrapersonal and Interpersonal Dimensions of Narcissism.' *PLOS ONE*. 9(4).

Mitra, P., Torrico, T.J. & Fluyau, D. (2024). 'Narcissistic Personality Disorder.' In: StatPearls [Internet]. Treasure Island (FL): StatPearls Publishing; 2025 Jan.

Tagoe, T. (2023). 'The effect of narcissistic leadership on employee workplace flourishing.' University of Wollongong. Thesis.

Burnout, Trauma and Wellbeing

Kessler, R.C., Aguilar-Gaxiola, S., Alonso, J., Benjet, C., Bromet, E.J., Cardoso, G. et al. (2017). 'Trauma and PTSD in the WHO world mental health surveys.' *European Journal of Psychotraumatology*, 8(sup5).

Mental Health UK (2025). 'Burnout Report 2025.'

Walker, P. (2013). *Complex PTSD: From Surviving to Thriving: A Guide and Map for Recovering from Childhood Trauma* (Paperback). CreateSpace Independent Publishing Platform.

World Health Organization (2019). 'Burn-out "an occupational phe-nomenon": International Classification of Diseases.'

Mindfulness, Meditation and Psychological Health

Cherkin, D.C. et al. (2016). 'Effect of mindfulness-based stress reduction vs cognitive behavioral therapy or usual care on back pain and functional limitations.' *JAMA*, 315(12), 1240–49.

Goyal, M., et al. (2014). 'Meditation programs for psychological stress and well-being.' *JAMA Internal Medicine*, 174(3), 357–68.

Hölzel, B.K. et al. (2011). 'Mindfulness practice leads to increases in regional brain grey matter density.' *Psychiatry Research: Neuroimaging*, 191(1), 36–43.

Kabat-Zinn, J. (1994). *Wherever You Go, There You Are: Mindfulness Meditation in Everyday Life*. Hyperion.

Keng, S.L., Smoski, M.J. & Robins, C.J. (2011). 'Effects of mindfulness on psychological health: a review of empirical studies.' *Clinical Psychology Review*, 31(6), 1041–56.

Ong, J.C. et al. (2014). 'A randomized controlled trial of mindfulness meditation for chronic insomnia.' *Sleep*, 37(9), 1553–63.

Classic and Theoretical Works

Emerald, D. (2005). *The Power of TED*. Polaris Publishing.

Karpman, S. (1968). *The Drama Triangle*. [Original work; see also later summaries.]

Kübler-Ross, E. (1969). *On Death and Dying*. Macmillan.